"If you have picked up this book, you are probably frustrated and looking for some answers. After teaching parenting for over 30 years, this is by far the most helpful, practical book I have read on ADHD. If you are tired of yelling, threatening, taking away privileges, and bribing, then this book is a must-read."

> —Kathryn Kvols, author of *Redirecting Children's Behavior* and
> president of the International Network for Children and Families

"A practical, non-judgmental guide for parents seeking an alternative to medication."

> —L. Alan Sroufe, PhD, professor at the Institute of Child
> Development, University of Minnesota, and author of
> *The Development of the Person*

"I highly recommend this book for all educators who are seeking alternative methods to work with students who test the boundaries of behavior. Craig B. Wiener gives us examples and insights to assist us in understanding why and how some children who were previously described as having "conditions" can be worked with using techniques that can modify unacceptable behaviors. This book supports the Montessori method, which also endorses doing the hard work necessary to help the child for the long term. I suggest to anyone interested in positive results to put in the time and effort with methods that are outlined in Wiener's new book."

> —Christine Kovago, director at Pincushion Hill Montessori School

Parenting Your Child *with* ADHD

A No-Nonsense Guide
for Nurturing Self-Reliance
and Cooperation

CRAIG B. WIENER, EdD

New Harbinger Publications, Inc.

Publisher's Note

Distributed in Canada by Raincoast Books

Copyright © 2012 by Craig B. Wiener
New Harbinger Publications, Inc.
5674 Shattuck Avenue
Oakland, CA 94609
www.newharbinger.com

Acquired by Jess O'Brien; Cover design by Amy Shoup;
Edited by Will DeRooy; Text design by Tracy Carlson

Library of Congress Cataloging-in-Publication Data

Wiener, Craig.
  Parenting your child with ADHD : a no-nonsense guide for nurturing self-reliance and cooperation / Craig B. Wiener.
       p. cm.
  Includes bibliographical references.
  ISBN 978-1-60882-396-3 (pbk. : alk. paper) -- ISBN 978-1-60882-397-0 (pdf e-book) -- ISBN 978-1-60882-398-7 (epub)
  1. Attention-deficit-disordered children. 2. Attention-deficit-disordered children--Behavior modification. 3. Parenting. I. Title.
  RJ506.H9W523 2012
  618.92'8589--dc23

                              2012024164

Printed in the United States of America

14 13 12   10 9 8 7 6 5 4 3 2 1   First printing

In memory of my parents, Morton and Beatrice

To my wife, Patricia, and sons, Scott and Casey

We were preparing for the Monday evening ADHD clinic. The first person to register was the mother of a boy about five years old. Sporting a T-shirt that advertised, "Here comes trouble!" he darted about in the reception area. As we tried to settle the family in the office, the mother, looking tired and discouraged, started to tell us the boy's story. While we attended to her, "Trouble" snatched a jar of pencils and pens off a table and watched them spill on the floor. He monitored his mother's look of helplessness and smirked. The therapist and I exchanged glances, and the mother burst into tears.

—Rosemary Quagan

Contents

Acknowledgments

A special thanks to Wendy Millstine, NC, at New Harbinger Publications for asking me to write this book after seeing my ADHD presentation at a recent American Psychological Association convention. Her support and encouragement were extremely helpful.

My appreciation also goes out to Jess O'Brien and the editorial staff at New Harbinger Publications. They truly give expert advice. When coupled with the enthusiasm of the marketing department, the entire project has been an author's dream.

I would also like to thank Rosemary Quagan, my colleague at Family Health Center of Worcester, for her assistance and friendship. And I applaud Will DeRooy for his very intelligent copyediting. If you have a manuscript that you would like to improve, give this man a call.

Introduction

This book is meant for parents of children diagnosed with attention deficit/hyperactivity disorder (ADHD), whether or not their child is already receiving treatment. It will help you understand ADHD in a new way and put you on a different course with your child. You will discover new ways to keep ADHD behavior from happening, and you will help your child more successfully meet expectations on his own and when interacting with others. You will learn that ADHD is not a permanent health impairment. ADHD is something that your child *does* rather than something that he *has*. It's a pattern of behavior, not a medical condition.

Have you noticed that your child is much less hyperactive, impulsive, and inattentive when engaged in an activity that he initiates and enjoys? Perhaps, for example, he can play with interlocking blocks for hours on end if left to himself. Time for self-directed play is very important to children, and they may not like having to adapt to limits on their behavior and requirements that they do other things. When directed or pressured to behave in certain ways, children may feel uncomfortable, and this discomfort makes ADHD behavior more likely. Unfortunately, it's necessary to place limits and requirements on children, because they have not yet learned about the dangers and the necessities of life.

So how do you establish ways of interacting that are comfortable for both of you? How do you get your child to cooperate without a hassle when he wants to do something else? How can you help him gradually assume responsibility and independence when he likes to have you do things for him? How can you get him to follow through when no one is watching over him?

As you read this book, you will see that it's not all that hard. But be prepared to be patient. Whereas threats and demands can produce instant conformity, helping your child learn self-reliance and cooperation is vastly superior but can take significantly more time. Occasionally, you may be unsure whether your efforts are working. For example, when your child throws a tantrum and you do not react, you are essentially permitting the unwelcome behavior in the short term. But your reluctance to feed into the drama may prove very effective in the long term.

You might also wonder whether you are being too lenient or whether you are letting your child get away with misbehavior when you use this new style of parenting. You might think that you are being negligent or that you are not doing all you can to eliminate his problems. However, the strategies in this book are not permissive at all. As you put them into use, you may find that you are being more assertive and firm than you have been. And the earlier you start the better.

This book will help you ease your child into more mature behavior. Eventually, he will do more on his own rather than depend on your reminders. He will give more consideration to others' feelings and behave in ways that make life easier for both of you.

When you put this new style of parenting into practice, you will take one or more of the following four actions. These parenting behaviors make up the foundation of the method, so keep them in mind. They are your basic tools, and you will learn how to use them throughout this book.

The Foundation of the New Approach

- Make changes that discourage ADHD behavior.

- Promote acceptable behavior with the least amount of coercion.

- Increase your child's self-help skills to decrease his dependency on you and others.

- Help your child recognize the negative side effects of ADHD behavior.

1

So Your Child Has an ADHD Diagnosis

Your child did not come with a manual. Parenting can be a difficult job to begin with, and now you face the difficult task of managing a child diagnosed with ADHD. Many people, laypersons and professionals alike, may be offering you advice, and you may hear many different ideas about what is wrong with your child. Whom do you believe? What is best to do?

The Usual Beginning

Most often, the story goes like this: A school-age child continually is disruptive in class and doesn't follow instructions. The teacher suggests to the parents that the child be evaluated for ADHD. The parents are not surprised—they have been concerned because the child has also been difficult to handle at home. Frequently the child seems to be "driven by a motor" and "out of control."

Perhaps as an infant, the child would shriek and be difficult to soothe. Maybe the child had a health problem or developmental delay that made it difficult for her to meet expectations. Perhaps she was very active and seemed to have a short attention span when she was a toddler, picking up toys only to quickly lose interest in them. For years, the parents might have worried that there was something wrong, and now others are telling them that it's ADHD.

It's interesting that so many of our children (especially boys) receive this diagnosis. According to a 2009 report by the U.S. Department of

Health and Human Services (Akinbami et al. 2011), an alarming 9 percent of our children ages four to seventeen receive an ADHD diagnosis. Is it because these children spend too much time in front of TV and computer screens instead of socializing? Are boys naturally more active and harder to settle down at home and in school? Is there not enough discipline in our families? Are we too concerned with making our children happy and not teaching them enough about limits? Are we too busy to be effective? Are we so concerned about safety that we are hindering the development of self-direction and independence for many of our children? Or are we simply getting better at identifying impaired children because of improvements in our health care system?

The Presumption of Impairment

Many people believe that ADHD equates to a lasting developmental disability that will affect a person throughout her life. Some people speculate that those with ADHD are *less able* to stop, look, listen, and think before they act (Douglas 1972). The specific criteria for ADHD are found in the *Diagnostic and Statistical Manual of Mental Disorders* (*DSM*) (American Psychiatric Association 2000). This manual lists the hyperactive, impulsive, and inattentive behaviors that children must show to receive the ADHD label.

There could be many different reasons for children to display the behaviors listed in the *DSM*. But it's now very common to think of ADHD as a biological delay caused by genetics, much like height or color-blindness. This leads us to be of the mind that the afflicted must accept their fate. They must live with the stigma of having a body that is inferior to others. Their delay will cause them to make careless errors, and they will have greater difficulty organizing, planning, and paying attention. They will be less able to complete tasks, follow directions, manage daily responsibilities, and remember what they are supposed to do.

Many professionals now recommend medication and stringent discipline for children with ADHD. It's believed that because it's unlikely that children with ADHD are mindful of the longer-term benefits of cooperation, the adults in their world must provide them with immediate rewards and punishments to coax them to meet expectations. They must oversee and remind the children throughout the day so that they will conform to social standards, one step at a time. In this view, however, there is no cure: children with ADHD will never be able to "put on the brakes" like others.

Starting Treatment

The ADHD diagnostic system and recommended therapies can be stressful and confusing. If your child has been diagnosed with ADHD, you might like it if she were more independent, but that may now seem like an impossible dream. If you start the recommended treatments, however, you will likely notice that the medications and strict discipline very quickly enhance her concentration and help her productivity skyrocket.

You might also see immediate improvements when your child receives accommodations in school. The organizational aids, reminders, extra time to complete tasks, extra books, and additional rewards and punishments to produce achievement will likely ignite welcomed behaviors. When she finishes her assignments and shows good conduct, you may wish you had started the recommended treatments even earlier.

The Downside of Looking at ADHD in This Way

Although there appear to be immediate and positive changes when you follow the usual recommendations, the strategies will not help your child learn self-reliance and cooperation. So you will never find out whether she can. You may even be creating undesirable side effects that you are unaware of when you function as a warden who pressures your child into compliance by doling out or pulling back resources that are important to her.

With this treatment, a child may begin to learn a variety of ways to counteract the attempts to govern her or come to rely on her parents even more to make sure she does what she is supposed to do. Instead of caring about her relationship with her mother and father, she may begin to focus more on the rewards they control. She may not learn about the joy of working together without an expected payment, and this will affect her relationships throughout her life.

Another concern looms as well: how do children with ADHD learn to self-manage? Stringency and supervision force them to comply, but that kind of parenting does not help them develop independence. And if no one is helping these children learn to behave acceptably without medication, pressure, and supervision, how can we ever expect them to? Because they will be more difficult to monitor as they grow older, this concern increases as children approach adolescence.

Potential Drawbacks of Medication

The decision to medicate your child is between you and your child's doctor. You may decide to use medication only, or you may find that it makes sense to use it in conjunction with other forms of therapy. Medication will very likely calm your child down and get her to focus and do her work. However, medication can have drawbacks that are not always evident right away.

Prescribers will assure you that ADHD medicines are powerful yet harmless, but how much of any medication is entirely safe? Side effects could worsen over time, and biological and psychological changes can become difficult to reverse the longer a drug remains in the body. Already there are reports that ADHD drugs can take a toll on the brain (Higgins 2009), and long-term effects on very young children are still unknown (Rappley 2006).

Medicinal treatment can also take away the urgency of a problem. Urgency is what drives people to work hard and change, and lack of urgency can lessen your desire to seek counseling for your child. You may end up relying solely on the medications. But what if the medications stop working?

Postponing psychotherapy can make things significantly more difficult. When children are older, it's not as easy for them to change their habits and routines. The saying comes to mind, "You can't teach an old dog new tricks."

Keeping your child on long-term medicinal treatment can also mean higher dosages and multiple drugs as time passes. Your child may need more medication as she grows, and there is a possibility that her body will build up a tolerance to the drug as well. Sadly, the potential for side effects increases with the amount and number of drugs needed to achieve the desired effects.

Medicinal therapy also may create the belief that medication is necessary for success, when in fact there might be other ways to resolve problems. Individuals may learn to seek psychiatric drugs as a primary way to make improvements in their lives and never explore whether they might resolve their problems in a different way.

It's also difficult to stop medicinal treatment once it's begun (even when supervised by a physician). Stopping medication means your child has to adjust psychologically and biologically to not having a chemical boost in her body. Unwanted behaviors will occur as soon as you withdraw the medication, and then you are "back to square one."

But most important, while medicinal therapy is certainly a reasonable treatment option when the benefits clearly outweigh the harm, the *long-term* advantages of ADHD medications have not been outstanding. Even staunch advocates of medicinal therapy acknowledge that medicinal therapy during childhood does not produce superior longer-term outcomes when children become adults (Barkley, Murphy, and Fischer 2008).

A case in point is the massive MTA Cooperative Group study on ADHD. While the initial results (1999) indicated that medication was the best treatment, later results showed that the benefits did not last. In as little as three years, medicated children were no longer behaving better than children who had received other treatments (MTA Cooperative Group 2004).

According to William Pelham (2007), a major contributor to the MTA study, ADHD medications are not superior treatments. Pelham is concerned that ADHD medications can have negative effects on a child's height and weight. He believes that medication should play a lesser role in the treatment of ADHD (Munsey 2008).

Decisions

So what does all of this mean? You can give your child stimulant medication and know that most of the time you will see immediate and significant improvements. However, there is the likelihood that the progress will be short-lived. Relying solely on medications may be ill-advised in the end even though the drugs can take away problems in a relatively quick and uncomplicated way.

There may be occasions, however, when a medication could be helpful for short-term use. Maybe your child's problems are so severe that it's imperative you seek quick relief. Maybe it will be easier to start teaching your child self-reliance and cooperation when she is in a medicated state. And maybe some of the improvements that you get from medicinal treatments will continue, if you decide to reduce and eventually eliminate the medications down the road. Just be aware that medicinal treatment has potential risks and shortcomings.

A New Understanding and Treatment for ADHD

Given the new information cautioning us on the use of medication to manage ADHD, it's time to examine ADHD through a different lens and use an entirely different approach to the problem—time for what scientists would refer to as a "paradigm shift." Doubtless you have noticed times when your child displays focus and follows directions without medication or stringent discipline. Her diagnosis means only that she is not doing these behaviors often enough at the expected times.

This book offers a new understanding of ADHD. You will no longer believe that your child has a medical problem that keeps her from meeting the standards that others impose but does not keep her from pursuing her own interests. You probably already know that your child is more competent than others would have you believe. If you could help her complete required work with the same flair and effort that she shows with tasks that she values and enjoys, that would improve the lion's share of her problems.

For example, many children with ADHD can remember that a certain food is in the refrigerator but not remember to close the kitchen drawer after taking out a fork to eat it with. Many are often reckless and loud when their parent is on the phone but as quiet as a mouse if the phone call delays their bedtime. Many will say that they do not know how to organize their room, but many of these same children can organize their action figures into intricate battle scenes. Many will forget homework but not forget to bring trading cards to school to show their friends. Many will blurt out inappropriate things that turn heads but not make a peep when their parents want them to admit wrongdoing. Many drift off task when writing thank-you notes but work feverishly when writing Christmas lists. And many will be lackadaisical with chores but set the table perfectly when buttering up their parents for a favor.

All of this may make you wonder whether there can really be a biological problem that operates in the way ADHD operates. If your child's delays were biological, her problems with self-management would be consistent and not so tightly linked to particular situations. ADHD is considered to be equivalent to needing glasses or a hearing aid (Monastra 2005), but what seeing or hearing problem disappears when a person is not interested in having it? It comes as no surprise that parents have been asking professionals for years, "Why can my child function so well when she is doing what she wants to do?"

Perhaps it's a good idea to return to a psychological perspective on the issue. What if, instead of being due to inborn differences in brain structure or chemistry, ADHD behavior is something your child has learned? Let's assume that in your child's experience, in certain situations, this kind of behavior yields a beneficial result.

When the outcome of a behavior has a beneficial effect, psychologists refer to this as *reinforcement* because it reinforces, or strengthens, the behavior, making it more likely to occur again. Can you identify some of the benefits or advantages that your child gets when she shows ADHD behavior?

Keep in mind that what may be reinforcing to your child may not be what you would consider desirable or in her best interest. The reinforcement can consist of her either receiving something she likes or getting rid of something she does not like. In this way of thinking, you can change your child's behavior by changing the way she profits when she shows ADHD behavior.

The table below will help you begin the process of understanding ADHD as something that your child *does* rather than something that she *has*. The first column describes ADHD behavior in the usual way. The second column links that behavior with psychological meaning and profit.

The child who *has* ADHD...	The child who *does* ADHD...
...is unable to listen when spoken to directly. ...does not follow through as instructed.	...does not want to comply.
...has difficulty sustaining attention. ...is easily distracted.	...disengages to avoid displeasure. ...daydreams. ...avoids expectations.
...is disorganized. ...is forgetful.	...sidesteps the work of putting things away in designated places. ...depends on others to manage.
...is driven by a motor. ...talks excessively. ...has difficulty remaining seated. ...has difficulty remaining quiet.	...is energetic and curious. ...likes attention. ...resists confinement.
...blurts out. ...interrupts. ...has difficulty awaiting her turn.	...is striking back. ...is contesting limits. ...likes to be noticed. ...enjoys creating a stir. ...does not want to miss out or be excluded.
...is impulsive.	...is irritable. ...is frustrated. ...is desperate for control or relief. ...is indulgent, intrusive, or showing off.
...makes careless mistakes.	...rushes to finish. ...likes to be first. ...is minimally compliant. ...depends on others to correct her mistakes.

…fidgets and squirms.	…is uncomfortable with restriction and evaluation.
	…wants to escape.
…has problems with tasks requiring mental effort.	…relies on others.
	…avoids failure.
	…is reluctant to exert the effort.

The Next Step

I'm guessing by now that you're excited about nurturing your child's self-reliance and cooperation. However, because many people believe that ADHD is a permanent disability, you may want to see that view refuted before you proceed on this new course. The next chapter aims to do just that.

2 Understanding ADHD Behavior as Reinforced

The first thing to realize is that while you and other adults see your child's ADHD behavior as a problem to overcome, for your child, ADHD behavior holds *solutions* to the difficulties that he faces on a daily basis. When your child encounters adversity, ADHD behavior somehow mitigates the situation. When you identify what gives his ADHD behavior its staying power, you will have gained valuable insight into why such behavior repeats so frequently. You will also be taking a giant step forward in knowing how to eliminate it.

In plain English, learning means *repeating what works*. When you have success doing something in a certain way, the next time you are in that situation, you will probably do the same thing again. For example, when you find out that pushing a particular button turns on an appliance, the next time you want to use the appliance, you go right for that button. While you might think there can't possibly be reinforcement for ADHD behavior, just wait and see.

Conformity and Accommodation

In the broadest sense, ADHD behavior is more likely when your child confronts hardship. Hardship for a child may take many different forms. One type of hardship for your child is when he must conform to someone else's limits and expectations. ADHD behavior is far less likely when your child is doing something he enjoys. When your child is comfortable and satisfied, ADHD behavior may seem to disappear.

This is why your child is unlikely to be hyperactive, impulsive, or inattentive when he is doing what he wants to do. When your child is in charge, he can operate at his own pace and please himself. When the activity is his own, he is not anxious about meeting expectations. He does not have to fulfill someone else's desires. He can start and stop when he wants. He does not feel trapped by the demands and limits of others, so there will be less squirming and discomfort. When he follows his own lead, he proceeds only when he is ready; he does not have to expose himself to unwanted risks. He has much more control over what happens in comparison to doing tasks assigned and evaluated by others.

Infants are not required to meet the demands of others, so these problems do not occur early in life. But toddlers and young children must achieve and conform to a greater degree. As your child grows older, expectations increase, and this can lead to conflicts of interest. What others want of your child may differ from what your child wants.

Some children show ADHD behavior when resolving the problem of *who will accommodate to whom*. Conflicts occur when they have to wait, share, transition, or allow others to go first. They lag in taking on responsibility, and they are less likely to conform to others' demands, wishes, and desires. They overreact when they lose and are intolerant when they do not get their way. Their actions create both social and academic problems because they are not adequately adjusting to what others expect. The behavior is consistent with what we expect from toddlers when they first respond to limits and boundaries. So the important question is: why do some children continue to behave so immaturely?

Accommodation in Groups

Groups are breeding grounds for ADHD behavior, because children often have problems accommodating when they must function in groups. In group settings, individuals are typically less important than the group as a whole, so they may feel neglected in comparison to one-on-one interactions, in which they have more influence and importance. It comes as no surprise, then, that one-on-one interaction results in less ADHD behavior in comparison to when a child is part of a group. This is why your child might have been doing okay before he started preschool or kindergarten.

When your child feels neglected or denied in a group, ADHD behavior can be quite effective in getting people to shift their attention back to him. When he doubts that he can fulfill group expectations, ADHD behavior also becomes probable. He may drop out from the activity and begin to tap and fidget. Soon he has disrupted the whole group from doing the activity, and someone must stop him from being a distraction. The advantages are clear even though the behaviors are difficult for the person in charge.

The Basic Solution

It's important to create acceptable resolutions to conflicts of interest. When you and your child are considerate toward each other, things go more smoothly and everyone is more likely to be calm and satisfied. For example, if your child learns to look out the window of his friend's house when it's time for you to pick him up, you will not mind allowing him to visit, and you will be happy to pick him up. The process is easier for you because you will not have to park the car and ring the bell to get him.

Your child's possibilities for success will increase if he learns to show greater concern for others. His caring behaviors will work well with his teachers, friends, romantic partners, and employers. Finding the balance between self-interest and consideration for others is never easy, but it's an important skill every parent should teach their child and a great way to eliminate ADHD behavior.

Benefits and Side Effects

Clearly, ADHD behavior creates many annoyances. It puts children at odds with others and breeds failure. So why do children continue to do these things, if they lead to so many harmful effects and difficulties?

The answer is that there are benefits even though there are side effects, which is true for most of our behaviors. For example, choosing to save rather than spend may prepare you for a comfortable retirement but make you less happy in the meantime. Choosing to read rather than exercise may make you more knowledgeable but contribute to health problems. Doing something fun might not leave you enough time to fulfill your obligations. And you might like it when others do things for you but dislike the loss of control that occurs when others make all the decisions.

In the same way, when your child shows ADHD behavior with schoolwork, his grades may suffer, but he also avoids the hardship of expending effort and still "coming up short." He may also mobilize a great deal of concern from teachers and other significant adults in the process. Your child may not directly be saying no to the challenges of learning and socialization—as someone who is oppositional or defiant might—but nevertheless he is not conforming. ADHD behavior is usually very successful here. It gets others to assist your child and lower their expectations. If allowed, the behavior can rule to the point where it's impossible for others to impose any kind of limit or demand.

Do Parents Cause ADHD Behavior?

Many parents ask, "If ADHD behavior is reinforced, does this mean that I caused my child's ADHD behavior?" The answer is that ADHD behavior is no one's fault. Saying that there is reinforcement for ADHD behavior does not imply that you or anyone else is doing something wrong. Usually many factors are in play.

Parents do not cause ADHD behavior, TV and video games do not cause ADHD behavior, and our culture does not cause ADHD behavior. If you put a group of people in the exact same environment, they would show many different responses and patterns of learning. Surroundings do not fully determine what people do. People often respond and profit in very different ways when operating under very similar conditions.

For example, a parent or teacher approaches a child who is distracted and not doing his schoolwork, in an effort to get him to cooperate. If the child highly values any kind of attention from the adult, however—even negative attention—this response by the adult may, counterintuitively, reinforce the distracted behavior. That is not the adult's intention—the adult is trying to put a stop to the ADHD behavior, in a way that might indeed have the desired effect with another child. It's therefore unreasonable to say that the adult is causing the problem.

Is ADHD Behavior On Purpose?

Saying that there is reinforcement for ADHD behavior does not mean that your child necessarily knows the benefits of his actions, has a sense of control over his behavior, or *wants* to show ADHD behavior. He may not be planning to get particular reactions from others or even be aware of what typically occurs when others observe ADHD behavior.

Often people are oblivious of the reinforcements associated with their behavior, and sometimes they consult professionals to help them learn to behave differently. It usually takes much effort to piece together why we do the things we do. Your child may not know what reinforces his ADHD behavior, just as you may not know what you can do to stop the reinforcement.

Proceeding without Blame

A psychological understanding of ADHD behavior does not imply that someone is to blame. A parent's behavior can lead to very different outcomes depending on the child, and similar child behaviors can influence parents in a wide variety of ways. A learning model is a dynamic process for both of you. What occurs over time is a result of many different factors coming together, and the mix of participants has a lot to do with the outcomes.

It's your job to identify the advantages that the behavior has for your child and then help him learn better alternatives. And I will help you do this. You did not cause your child's ADHD behavior, but you can do something about it. You can influence what he learns and, over time, help his ADHD behavior subside. Very young children at risk for ADHD behavior can benefit in remarkable ways from parenting interventions (Kern et al. 2007), and that is what you are going to do.

Biological Causality

The evidence supporting a biological cause for ADHD is not as strong as it first appears. The entire view rests on three research findings. First, professionals have identified genes that increase the risk of ADHD. Second, people diagnosed with ADHD exhibit different brain biology when compared to others. Third, medication, which changes biology, often eliminates the troublesome behaviors instantaneously. These findings seem impressive, but let's take a closer look at each one.

Genetics

The first aspect of the biological argument is that your child's genetic constitution causes his ADHD. Researchers claim that genetics increases the likelihood of ADHD by 50 percent (Barkley 2006). While this sounds remarkable, statistics like these can be misleading. A 50 percent increase means that the likelihood of ADHD increases from 9 percent to 13.5 percent if the child has certain genes. This small increase is hardly a reason to think that ADHD is inevitable when your child has a particular genetic constitution.

The genetic account is actually quite limited. Many people not diagnosed with ADHD have the genetic constitution associated with ADHD. There are also many people diagnosed with ADHD who do not have the suspected genes. Even though it's enticing to think that we are discovering the basic cause of ADHD when genes link with the diagnosis, the explanation is incomplete.

Yes, there is a slight increase in risk when a person has particular genes, but much can happen along the way to change whether your child eventually qualifies for the ADHD diagnosis. The challenge, of course, is to identify the factors that can influence ADHD behavior for your child no matter what kind of biology he possesses.

Brain Differences

The second aspect of the biological view is that people with ADHD tend to show differences in their brains compared with people without

ADHD. Many people think that this means that ADHD occurs *because* of these biological differences. However, correlation or association is not the same as causation. These findings do not tell us whether the biological differences cause ADHD behavior or whether they are the consequences of doing ADHD behavior for long periods. That is, the actions of these individuals may be influencing the development of their brain biology in observable ways.

A person's lifestyle can affect brain chemistry, brain response, and the size of certain parts of the brain. For example, your child's brain can grow differently if he plays a musical instrument (Gaser and Schlaug 2003). And children diagnosed with ADHD can alter their patterns of brain functioning and alertness using biofeedback (Wright 2001; Monastra 2005). This shows that brain functioning is malleable, not static or fixed. This quality is called *neuroplasticity*, and very young children (including those with ADHD) possess it in large amounts.

If your child is frequently unenthusiastic when you make requests of him, those responses are bound to have an effect on his brain's alertness. If others frequently solve problems for him, he will have less development of the frontal lobes, the region of the brain that governs problem solving and complex decision-making. If he often gets his way when he reacts excessively, his brain will activate and develop differently than if he had not been reinforced in that manner. These sorts of daily experiences are often overlooked, however, by professionals searching for internal biological causes.

The Power of Medication

The third and final basis of the biological argument is that medication works in the case of ADHD because it corrects a problem caused by an inept body. Even though most people who take ADHD drugs get a performance boost from them, the public in general and many professionals think that the drugs are effective because they compensate for some kind of biological deficiency, much as insulin injections help people with diabetes. The drugs change biology, so they conclude that a faulty biology must be the source of the problem.

But there are difficulties with that interpretation. For example, alcohol might help a person become more social, but that does not tell us why he was not social. Aspirin might help a person with a headache, but that does not tell us why he got a headache. Radiation can help a person with cancer, but that does not tell us that he has a radiation deficiency. The point is that the treatment may not tell us very much about the cause of the problem.

A New Way to Understand Biology and ADHD

As you may already know, children diagnosed with ADHD are more likely to show developmental delays, coordination disorders, specific speech and learning problems, health complications, short attention spans, high activity levels, and demanding and intense infant responses (Barkley 2006). Those who believe that ADHD is a biological delay are not surprised here. They know that we need a capable body to operate effectively, and they conclude that children with ADHD do not operate effectively because they have less competent bodies.

This point of view may seem reasonable, but there are other possible interpretations. One is that problematic traits and dysfunctions may occur with ADHD because *children with particular kinds of difficulties are more likely to learn ADHD behaviors*. For example, a child may be less inclined to participate when success is unlikely. He may not believe that he can meet standards through his own effort and may become frustrated or stop trying. He may also learn to rely on his parents and may have difficulty when they are not readily available.

Parents as well may be less inclined to foster their child's independence and self-discipline when their child is difficult, needy, or at risk. They would more likely impose on the child and take over management responsibilities. Once these interactions begin, the child's self-regulatory skills will lag even more. A downward spiral may occur, creating an even greater necessity for loved ones to compensate and take over.

It's clear that biology creates consequences for learning. If a child is very short and uncoordinated, he is unlikely to ever play professional basketball. There is no "basketball gene" that he lacks; it's just that people learn different behaviors when they have different kinds of biology. The short, uncoordinated child is likely to avoid playing basketball and spend his time doing things he is better at and more likely to find rewarding.

It's not surprising that ADHD runs in families and seems to have a genetic basis, as indicated in studies that show that if one identical twin receives an ADHD diagnosis, most likely the other will too (Faraone and Doyle 2001). We expect that family members will show similar behaviors. Family members tend to have similar bodies and environments, so they are likely to learn in similar ways. They are likely to experience similar kinds of problems and successes, and nowhere is this more true than in the case of identical twins.

Four Examples of Biology Increasing ADHD Behavior

Here are four examples of how early-occurring biological anomalies can increase the likelihood of a child's learning ADHD behavior. We begin with the story of Asif, which illustrates how infants who are difficult to console, irritable, and more easily angered in comparison to other infants (referred to as having *negative infant temperament*) are more likely to end up qualifying for an ADHD diagnosis (Barkley 1998).

• Asif's Story

Raising Asif was stressful from the beginning. Because of his negative temperament, it was necessary for his parents to go to great lengths to soothe him when he was upset. Rarely did he gain composure on his own, and he ended up being reliant on his parents' efforts to calm him down. Luckily, his parents found out that a long ride in the car would sedate him.

When Asif was in his preschool years, his family experiences were not positive. His short temper made it difficult for others to enjoy his company. When Asif did not get what he wanted, he would get angry and shout. To get him to stop shouting, his parents then would either give in to his demands or try to coerce him. The emotional intensity made everyone involved feel stressed and exhausted.

Clearly, Asif was not learning to respond calmly or find a middle ground when he related to others. Because of his prickliness and strong responses, it was difficult for him to adapt and get along with his family, peers, or teachers when he was old enough to attend school. His initial temperament set the stage for his eventual ADHD diagnosis.

Now let's take the example of Donald to illustrate how problems with coordination can increase ADHD behavior.

• Donald's Story

Donald had poor motor skills from birth onward. He did not learn to crawl during his first year, so he was completely dependent on his parents to hand him objects and carry him around. Because of his struggles, it was frequently necessary for Donald's parents to offer assistance. However, he learned it was easier to rely on his parents rather than try to manage for himself. He quickly learned to say "I can't" and wait for his parents' assistance. He learned to complain as soon as a task became hard, and he did not sustain achievement on his own. Instead of perseverance and self-management, he developed an overreliance on his parents.

Donald felt vulnerable and insecure when his parents were busy with other things. In addition, his parents were worried about a higher probability of accidents with him, so they usually liked to stay close to him, for their own peace of mind. Thus both Donald and his parents were apprehensive when they were not in close proximity, and this interfered with his independence. Donald learned a variety of behaviors to keep his parents focused on what he was doing. When he started school, his poor self-management and attention-provoking behavior easily qualified him for the ADHD diagnosis.

Because it was difficult for Donald to do things like bounce a ball or hop or skip, he did not feel competent to participate in physical activities in the classroom or on the playground. Because he doubted he could be successful, he learned to give up quickly. This saved him from embarrassment, but it also prevented him from improving his motor skills with practice.

Donald's coordination problems had a negative impact on his social life as well. This was readily apparent when others picked him last when organizing a sports team. Rarely did his peers invite him to play. In order to maintain his dignity, he was reluctant to join in and he pretended not to care. Because he doubted that his peers would include him, he sometimes went on the offensive. He pushed others away before they could reject him. This gave him some control over what he was experiencing, but he got a reputation for impulsivity. Like Asif, he was very disruptive.

Chang's case illustrates how early high activity levels can increase ADHD behavior for many children.

• Chang's Story

Compared to others, Chang had numerous mishaps. He burned himself when he crashed into his mother's ironing board, and he frightened her by going into the deep end of the pool. His mother had to intervene in his activities frequently in order to protect him, and the two of them got into many conflicts over limits. Eventually, in order to ensure his safety, she put him into a harness, but he learned to escape.

Chang's mother received constant disapproval from friends and family because it seemed like Chang was always breaking things and creating chaos. His high activity levels and recklessness put him at constant odds with his mother, and their relationship grew increasingly negative. Yet it seemed as if whenever she did anything except focus on him, his behavior worsened. He was monopolizing her attention and, it seemed, her life.

When Chang started kindergarten, he found it very uncomfortable and confining. The mismatch between his active behavior and the sedentary school setting made it difficult for him to succeed. Not surprisingly, he dreaded going to school each morning, and within the first few weeks of kindergarten, he received a diagnosis of ADHD.

• Dianne's Story

When Dianne was four years old, she still could speak only one or two words at a time. This made it difficult for others to know what she wanted and whether she understood them. Her primary way to provoke attention and relate to others was to zoom around her preschool classroom, touching materials and bothering other students. Not surprisingly, this was exhausting to the staff. When Dianne was in the room, it was difficult for them to give attention to the other students. She was unruly when a teacher was not sitting with her, and everyone thought that she should get professional help for her ADHD. Eventually she had to leave the preschool because the staff did not think they could manage her effectively.

It was easy for her parents to accept the view that something unique was going on with Dianne, because they did not have the same kind of problems with her seven-year-old sister, Isabella. Isabella was very articulate and very successful in school. She could work out problems with her parents by talking with them.

But in addition to the normal amount of sibling rivalry, Isabella resented that Dianne received extra attention as a result of her problems, and she often belittled Dianne. She frequently corrected Dianne and highlighted her incompetence when she tried to achieve. When Dianne received positive attention, Isabella criticized her even more, and this did not help Dianne's self-confidence or willingness to persevere. Isabella liked it when her parents were upset with Dianne, so she encouraged Dianne to misbehave. Conflict between Dianne and Isabella kept escalating, and their parents were caught in the middle.

Dianne's language delay created many obstacles and greatly influenced her development. Dianne was reliant on her parents to talk for her, and this increased her need to have them available. Because she was not expressing her desires verbally, she learned to intrude and overreact to make her wishes known. Her movements and touching became her way of relating, and she frequently created drama.

In family settings, she was often immature and silly, and that put her in the spotlight. Often when she did something that her parents and sister found objectionable, she would glance in their direction to see the troubled look on their faces. These behaviors distracted everyone from what they were doing, disrupting the entire family.

Due to her failure to communicate verbally, Dianne did not stay involved when the family gathered. She produced no input, so she did not participate. She went off by herself when her parents and sister were talking and did not stay current with family interactions. When she did the same behaviors at school, her teachers were discouraged. She rarely participated during group activities, and she missed many learning opportunities.

Because Dianne's parents had trouble knowing what she understood, it was difficult for them to hold her accountable when she failed to meet expectations. Sometimes they repeated instructions and became frustrated when she did not respond. On other occasions, they gave in and felt sorry for her. The inconsistency of their discipline slowed her progress. Doubts about her competence kept the family from placing age-appropriate demands on her, and she cried easily and often to get assistance from those around her. She liked it when others worked hard to understand what she wanted.

As you can see, Dianne was learning to interact negatively, extremely, and dependently. She was profiting from her ADHD behavior, but that behavior was having harmful side effects as well.

Asif, Donald, Chang, and Dianne had atypical behavior from the start. Their difficulties increased the likelihood of their learning ADHD behavior.

So What Can We Conclude?

It's understandable that high activity levels, short attention spans, and demanding and intense emotional responses all correlate with an eventual diagnosis of ADHD (Nigg, Goldsmith, and Sacheck 2004). Early patterns of maladaptive behavior are likely to disrupt social training and influence learning throughout childhood. It does not matter whether you are a birth parent or an adoptive parent; these conditions make it difficult for anyone to socialize a child, and they provide fertile ground for ADHD behavior.

Rather than think of ADHD as a biological problem, you can think of it as a particular way to operate in the world. Particular kinds of biology may increase the probability that your child will learn to operate in an ADHD way, but the outcome is not definite. You can do much to prevent ADHD behavior even when your child has the kinds of early-occurring biological problems associated with the diagnosis.

For example, Mary Jane Gandour (1989) emphasizes that highly active toddlers will benefit from a great deal of stimulation. This can substantially reduce their activity levels and patterns of rapid exploring. Always remember, not all active toddlers receive an ADHD diagnosis. Much can happen as your child grows and learns. There is no biological trait or early performance problem that *inevitably* leads to an ADHD diagnosis. And some children with ADHD start out as calm babies without developmental problems.

The Next Step

Your child can change (biologically and psychologically) depending on his experiences. He may have started out facing more adversity than others face, and this can make it more difficult for him to strike that delicate balance of give and take necessary for successful relationships and achievement. Nevertheless, he can learn to stand on his own two feet and interact in a more mature way. The next chapter will help you understand what gives ADHD its staying power. When you know precisely what triggers and fuels your child's ADHD behavior, it will be easier to halt it.

3 The Five Reinforcements for ADHD Behavior

Very young children are naturally self-centered. They are vulnerable, and they depend on others for security and support. Being able to command the attention of their caregivers is crucial for their survival. Thus they often find reinforcement for many hyperactive or impulsive behaviors: these behaviors typically draw people in and get things to happen quickly.

As children get older, they are expected to be more in control of themselves and to follow many rules. They tend to chafe at these restrictions on their behavior. That is when inattentiveness may come to be reinforced as a way to avoid "big kid" responsibilities.

In other words, ADHD behavior (hyperactivity, impulsivity, inattentiveness) can result in outcomes that relieve your child's discomfort. They can also get you and others to give your child more attention and assistance. When you understand what reinforces ADHD behavior, you can alter the consequences for this sort of behavior, to reduce its frequency. You can help your child learn different behaviors, ones that produce better outcomes with fewer negative side effects.

The Five "A"s

Your child's ADHD behavior may have any of the following beneficial effects: it may garner *attention* for her, it may get others to make *accommodations* for her, it may help her *avoid* certain situations, it may help her *acquire* something she wants, and it may *antagonize* others for doing things she does not like. Any one of the five "A"s can increase the frequency of ADHD behavior. Sometimes these reinforcements even work in combination to drive particular behaviors, strengthening them that much more.

Attention

Your child may become rambunctious as soon as you begin talking with a friend. This may happen because your involvement with someone else triggers insecurity in your child. She might begin to touch off-limits objects or make a noise as soon as your attention shifts away from her. These behaviors have the powerful effect of getting you to notice what she is doing. Sometimes an acknowledging smile or facial movement is all that it takes to encourage her to keep repeating this kind of ADHD behavior.

ADHD behaviors can be powerful ways to keep you focused on your child. It's difficult to separate from your child when she is loud, hyperactive, crazed, disagreeable, or intrusive. Putting objects close to your face or flopping roughly onto your lap when you are talking with someone can be an effective way to get your attention to shift.

Off-task behaviors at school or at home can draw a great deal of attention. When your child flounders, fiddles, or does not follow instructions, others may feel obligated to approach and stay with her until she complies. This may reassure her that others care and that they are concerned about her. Her negligence may lead to offers of help and encouragement, and she may like it when an adult repeats her name or pleads for a response. Her actions may even win her a special seat right next to you or her teacher.

Waiting rooms and other public places are fertile ground for attention-provoking behavior because your child has a captive audience. If you read a magazine to pass the time, this ADHD behavior can begin quickly. Your child is not being mean; she is simply keeping you engaged. Being loud and outlandish has many advantages. Often the loudest and most bizarre person in the room is the one who is most noticed. Shouting can be a way to increase the likelihood of a response; clowning can be entertaining, and it's generally more difficult for parents to enforce limits when others are watching.

People may say that your child cannot "hold back" as well as others, but the extreme behaviors have benefits we cannot ignore. When your child chatters and thinks aloud, she is certainly more noticeable. Her frequent talking keeps her from feeling lonely, and you always know what she is doing when you hear a running commentary. Her stream of talking and noise keeps both of you connected. She may go off on tangents, but her never-ending story leaves no room for anyone else to speak.

The drama created by attention-provoking behavior leaves little room for others. This does not necessarily mean that your child is not getting enough attention. It simply means that attention is beneficial, and some children like to get more attention than other children do. Practical jokes and various transgressions at school will usually make your child the hot topic when the family convenes later in the day. And going counter to your preferences can guarantee that she will remain the focus of your concerns.

Accommodation

ADHD behavior generally remits as soon as the child hears the word "yes." Loved ones will frequently offer relief when hearing a child complain or create problems. This can occur when your child overreacts, shows frustration, becomes self-critical, or behaves in any number of ways that indicate distress. When a child is diagnosed with ADHD and considered impaired, the tendency is for the adults in her life to lower their expectations and offer support.

ADHD behavior frequently results in social accommodation. For instance, if your child creates a scene because she wants you to leave, you unwittingly reinforce her impatience when you hurry along. If your child gets you to promise something extra to get her to calm down, her difficult behavior results in her getting more. Even if you threaten to punish, she is still learning not to comply until you spend extra time and energy. ADHD can be very effective in getting you to give more, do more, and work harder.

Another example of this problem occurs when your child is inattentive and then relies on you to inform her about what is happening. She is not learning to pay attention on her own. If she does this in school, she is unlikely to succeed. Her teachers will not have the time to constantly bring her up to speed.

Your child may also associate love with rescue. Your attempts to keep her from harm when she ventures into problematic or risky situations can reassure her that she is important to you. And this includes checking and reminding her about her basic self-care needs.

The accommodated child will often ask questions about matters that she can easily resolve on her own. She enjoys the fact that you drop everything to address her concerns. Playing dumb or foolish can increase assistance because it's difficult to impose requirements, hold her accountable, or ask her to contribute when you have doubts about her competence. Her staying ineffectual can keep you preoccupied with her, and it becomes your responsibility to solve her trials and tribulations. Often she will complain, "Why didn't you remind me?" when you failed to run interference for her. The side effect when you and others "pick up the slack" is that she remains unskilled.

If your child is accustomed to being the center of your worries and concerns, she may learn to be self-gratifying at others' expense. If she is accustomed to frequent pampering, she is unlikely to adapt to what others want. Showering her with easements during the course of the day or making a big deal about minor achievements (such as getting into the bath) could make it difficult for her to function in settings in which accommodation is less frequent.

All of this means that ADHD behavior is unlikely to diminish as long as social accommodation is excessive. A child exhibiting ADHD behavior can take over a family, as in Jack's example.

• Jack's Story

Jack was reluctant to compliment or show appreciation for his parents' attempts to please him. They desperately wanted to be good parents, because they came from families that expected a lot from them. They had worked hard to please their parents, and now they were working hard to please Jack. But Jack would not let them know that he was pleased. He did not want to feel obligated to give back to them, and his parents worked harder when he had a scowl on his face. Jack maintained control over his parents by making them feel like failures, and he would not let them off the hook. When Jack was dissatisfied, he was irritable and was aggressive with his younger brother, so his parents went to great lengths to make sure that he would not be upset. On some occasions, he would sabotage an activity that was not up to his expectations, and his parents would scurry around to make things better.

Often they were preoccupied with him throughout the day. Frequently, they arranged their lives to avoid annoying him. He continued to complain and pout despite their best efforts to make him happy, and he learned that his parents would cave to get him to stop. Whenever his parents reached their wits' end and yelled at him, he acted like a victim; then at the end of the day his parents felt guilty about losing their cool.

Unfortunately, Jack experienced significant disappointment when other people did not cater to him as his parents did, and this became a big problem when he started school. In that setting, his hot temper and his failure to conform did not get others to bend over backward to please him—those behaviors got him into constant trouble. Because he was accustomed to significant accommodations at home, he was not adequately prepared to function in a classroom environment. He had not yet learned to persist, withstand disappointment, or make an effort to keep others happy.

Not surprisingly, Jack resisted doing his homework. Often he would leave assignments and projects unfinished, and it took him hours to finish a small task for school. In an effort to keep him from failing, and to calm the drama, his parents sat with him and did much of the work for him.

While Jack enjoyed the fact that he could get his parents to shoulder most of his homework, the downside of this situation is obvious: he was not meeting expectations on his own. He received passing grades only because his parents worked so hard. His parents were certainly interested in helping him, but he was also learning many behaviors consistent with an ADHD diagnosis.

Why Parents Overaccommodate

Parents may frequently make accommodations on behalf of their child for many reasons. Sometimes parents feel that it's too dangerous not to shield the child. Whenever parents are anxious about potential risks, they are likely to err on the safe side. If they are prone to guilt, they are also more likely to overaccommodate. Single parents especially may over-accommodate due to guilt because the child has been through a divorce, because they feel that they have neglected the child because they have worked too many hours, or because the child has experienced abandonment from the other parent. Some parents are eager to please their child because of their own deprivation as children. These parents do not want their child to suffer as they have suffered. Some overaccommodate to ease a traumatized child's pain. They meticulously resolve problems so that the child will not have to endure additional hardships or risks. Some may excessively do for their child because they are rushed and have no time to let the child learn from her own mistakes. Some are concerned about not being good enough, and they excessively please to gain acceptance. And some take most of the responsibility in the household because that is what they learned to do when they were growing up. Whatever the reason or justification, overaccommodation can get in the way of the development of a child's self-management and willingness to meet others halfway.

We all may wish to make things easier for our children, but children must also learn that struggling is part of life. The difficulty, of course, is striking a balance between expecting too much and settling for too little. While you may be creating a bond with your child by doing something pleasing for her, you may be fostering behavior that will not allow her to function without your input. As parents, we may like it when our children feel close to us, secure, and cared for, but we also want them to develop self-reliance so that they can do for themselves when we are not around.

If you simplify a task or give your child clues to a solution before she has put in a reasonable amount of effort, you are being supportive, but she is not learning to exert herself. If you remind her to take her belongings, she might not learn to remember them without your prompt. And if you are eager to help her with her coat, it certainly saves time and makes things easier, but you also delay the time when she learns to put her coat on independently. On top of that, you may be creating quite a burden for yourself and grow to resent this arrangement in the future.

Avoidance

Avoidance is a very popular way for children and grown-ups alike to cope with adversity. The benefits of avoidance can perpetuate distractibility and lack of focus and listening, the hallmarks of ADHD. As Mark Twain (1897, 176) says, "It is easier to stay out than get out." However, when we avoid, we do not gain mastery, and the problem never goes away. Burying our heads in the sand like an ostrich is not good for any of us in the end.

Once a child has received the ADHD diagnosis, many people no longer try to understand the child's behavior as a failure to participate, join in, or conform. They believe that her ADHD keeps her from paying attention when spoken to. They think that she cannot learn to stop what she is doing and listen to what you say. When she keeps playing and fails to respond to your requests, they assume that it's because she is pathologically hyperfocused. People will stop saying that she is ignoring you; instead they will blame her lack of courtesy and awareness on her ADHD.

But all of these distracted responses have benefits as well. Often they can shield your child from difficulty and permit her to continue with *her* agenda. She may feel that others fail to listen to her, so she stops listening in return. This includes tuning others out or yawning when they are being critical or demanding. It includes changing the subject when they are pressing her to talk about certain topics. And it includes daydreaming and not acknowledging others.

Rather than having an inability, your child may have learned that when she does not respond, she does not have to submit to the requirement that you impose. Distractibility gives her more time to do what she wants. It permits her to float away on her imagination.

Distractibility protects a child from all kinds of discomfort. It pulls her away from situations associated with evaluation, correction, and restriction. Her immersion in her own thoughts and activity shields her from what is distasteful, including tasks that are too easy or redundant.

Your child may also become lethargic as soon as she thinks you are nagging or lecturing, and a tired look may sweep across her face. Most people know how difficult it is to listen to extended speaking without getting an opportunity to have input. If the speaking goes on long enough, many people may begin to show underarousal, and their brain biology will reflect the way they are responding. Children with ADHD are simply showing these kinds of reactions very often and very quickly.

Your child may seem incapable, lazy, and scatterbrained, but she is also escaping what disrupts her and withdrawing so that she does not have to hear something negative about herself or possibly experience a sense of failure. If she thinks that she must be perfect or doubts that others will be appreciative, she may be even less inclined to immerse herself and stay on task. In such cases the slightest sound in the room might draw her attention, although at other times—when she is comfortable with what she is doing—it would go unnoticed.

Perhaps your child often exhibits no understanding of something she has just read. But if she finds no pleasure in what she reads (or if something else preoccupies her), it's understandable that she drifts away while looking at the words. And perhaps when she insists that she is *unable* to concentrate, you stop reprimanding and pressuring her to fully engage with this sort of boring task, because then your efforts seem pointless.

Fidgeting with objects and squirming can also be signs of stress and a desire to escape. Often these behaviors indicate that a child feels disrupted by what is happening and wants to get away. She may insist that she cannot stay in her seat, but her hiding in the corner and taking forever to sharpen her pencil allow a prolonged escape from the work that she does not want to do.

Not organizing her materials and forgetting assignments can increase your child's time for play. She avoids the extra work of putting things away, and she sidesteps unwanted tasks. If you threaten her, she simply learns new ways to evade. If you demand that she listen, she may talk over you or maneuver so that you cannot get a word in edgewise.

The behaviors we call "impulsive" may also relate to avoidance. For example, when your child is bothered, she may start a commotion by doing something impetuous. She not only gets to let off steam, but also effectively distracts herself from what was troubling her.

A similar benefit occurs when your child goofs around, rambles, and entertains. While the behaviors provoke attention, they also distract others from whatever was taking place. This may effectively reduce family feuding or uncomfortable silences. Your child's actions may serve to bring down the level of stress.

Acquisition

Some ADHD behaviors enable a child to get things more quickly. The proverbs "Strike while the iron is hot" and "Get it while you can" illustrate the benefits of acting with urgency. Often the child who acts quickly will not miss out, because it's difficult for others to block rapid and intrusive goal-oriented behavior, such as pushing to the front to get the largest piece of cake. Many ADHD behaviors can prevent others from denying your child what she wants. Your child can swiftly obtain what she wants when her actions are abrupt and she does not stop to give others their turn.

We do not like it when children grab, touch excessively, behave rudely, act recklessly, or impose on others, but it's difficult to get these behaviors to stop when they work so well. Your child may ping-pong around the house looking for some sort of gratification, just like you do when you channel surf. ADHD behavior can usually speed things up and push limits to the side to help your child find pleasure more quickly. Impulsive behavior makes it difficult for others to anticipate her actions and stop her from getting what she desires.

Your child can also gain a sense of notoriety when she blurts out what others are afraid to say. It's not that she lacks a filter; it's that her actions increase her impact whether you like it or not. We try to encourage polite behavior, but sometimes a child misses out less often when she is impolite, and sometimes it's better to say "Sorry" than to ask for permission. We might think that the child lacks the ability to delay gratification or think before she acts, but this is only her ADHD behavior working all too well.

Your child can enjoy the fun of acquiring what she wants even if down the line there will be negative consequences. Her actions become even more advantageous if others rescue her or smooth things over when the future problems occur. That is why it's important to determine how often others bail her out before assuming that her rashness is a sign of impairment.

Antagonism

When your child is angry or upset, she may want to strike back. While some children fend for themselves assertively or aggressively, children diagnosed with ADHD are typically more indirect in response to conflict. For example, they might flick small objects in your direction or play recklessly with a household item. We call these behaviors impulsive, but they serve a purpose. They get you quite irritated, and that may suit the child just fine.

The stronger your reaction to the behavior in this case—the more exasperated and infuriated you become—the more likely the behavior will repeat. Your child will learn exactly how to "push your buttons." For example, when your child is angry about being forced to wait for an appointment, her embarrassing actions will have the effect of punishing you. While you might think that she blurts out because she is unable to control her impulses, that is not it at all. Her actions are potent ways to distress you for dragging her along.

It's not that she has difficulty "putting on the brakes." She is baiting and disrupting you when she creates a scene. She might flail around and repetitiously touch what you have forbidden her to touch. All of these actions can be annoying and function as retribution. She knows that showing unruliness in front of others bothers you, and she makes you self-conscious because you do not want to be seen as a bad parent.

Why Does Your Child Antagonize?

The responses I have just described indicate unresolved problems in the relationship. Identifying and solving those problems is crucial if your parenting is going to be effective. You want your child to deal with disappointment and conflict in positive ways. Antagonism only keeps the feud going.

Your child may not always be aware of what is bothering her, however. She might be instigating and disrupting without knowing what she is disturbed about, and you might not know either. Sometimes she may not be upset with you at all. She might be taking out her frustrations on you because you are "safe" or the first one available. Sometimes she might antagonize you simply because you failed to give her attention or refused a request.

It's not always easy to identify reasons for a child's antagonism. Relationships can be complex and difficult to untangle. Certain situations can trigger memories of old incidents and disrupt the current rapport that you have with your child.

Sometimes your child's overreacting may indicate that the problem has occurred on more than one occasion. It's troublesome for anyone to contend with problems that keep repeating, and your child may overreact at these times as well. For example, she may become unbearable when she thinks you are implying that she is untrustworthy, if that has been an ongoing issue between you.

Your child may also antagonize you when she feels that you are disinterested in including her. Her irritating behavior can be a way to gain dominance, and she avoids the risk of being nice and then getting disappointed. If she feels unwelcomed, she may retaliate by doing something disrespectful. This will force you to respond and make you suffer in the process. We all know that "misery loves company."

Rather than feeling teased and feeble, your child can do the hurting. She controls the rejection when she is bothering you or being obnoxious. Antagonizing can help her feel less vulnerable, and it can test whether you care enough to resolve her unhappiness and settle her down.

Antagonizing can also be disguised and roundabout. Your child may tell you that she will complete an assignment but then not follow through. She may do the assignment poorly, lose it, or not turn it in. Many children diagnosed with ADHD silently battle by not doing *what is important to their parents*, including schoolwork and household duties. Failing is their weapon, and they may act out their parents' worst fears. However, the battle usually leads to nothing positive. Your child achieves less and gets into jeopardy, while you become increasingly distressed.

A Frequent Benefit

You might wonder how all this conflict can possibly benefit your child. But the most important and frequent benefit of antagonism is the *making up* that occurs afterward. For example, you might regret that you overreacted and feel that you owe your child an apology. This may include pleasing and accommodating her in ways that would not otherwise occur. Your child may also want to patch things up after misbehaving, and you may have to stop what you are doing to attend to her request for forgiveness. Like most ADHD behavior, the result is that your child gains a monopoly on your time and energy.

On some occasions, however, your child may be reluctant to forgive you, which may result in your trying to please her even more. She may want other family members to console her, and she may hope to receive sympathy by telling them that you have been unkind. Think about your reaction when your child comes to you for support. Might it be reinforcing antagonistic behavior? Unfortunately, if others comfort her, they unknowingly undermine your attempts to discipline. Even though events began with your child creating what seemed to be needless trouble, they end with the tables completely turned. Everyone thinks that the problem is your fault. No wonder it's difficult to eliminate ADHD behavior.

Functional Assessment

When a child shows behavioral problems, it's not uncommon for a behavior specialist to come to the child's school or home and do an intervention called a *functional assessment* (Newcomer and Lewis 2004). Also called an *ABC analysis*, this involves figuring out how the *antecedent* (the situation that comes before), the unwanted behavior, and its consequences create a dynamic that works for your child. You can do a very similar intervention with your child by identifying the reinforcements for her ADHD behaviors.

Identifying situations and consequences gives you two different ways to eliminate your child's ADHD behavior. First, when you know the situations that ignite ADHD behavior, you can proactively make changes so that problems are resolved ahead of time. For example, you can leave your child with a babysitter instead of taking her to an antique store, or you can include your child in a conversation with your friend instead of ignoring her until she interrupts. Second, you can identify your reactions that increase ADHD behavior and stop reacting in those ways. For example, you can make sure your child's rambunctious behavior does not get you to shorten your phone call.

Exercise: Identify What Reinforces ADHD Behavior for Your Child (All Ages)

Practice identifying how your child might be profiting from ADHD behavior. Read the following examples of ADHD behavior in specific situations. In the right hand column, write down the reinforcement that seems to be at work for each example. After you finish, check the answer key below the table.

ADHD behavior and your response	Reinforcement
1. Your child is dancing in front of a stranger in a waiting room while you are reading a magazine. You ask her to come to you and look at pictures in the magazine you are reading.	
2. Your child is groaning and covering her face while doing her homework. You go over to her desk and ask her whether she needs help.	
3. Your child sticks out her leg and trips her younger brother. You yell at her. She runs to her room and you rush in to talk.	
4. Your child reaches quickly to get food before others and knocks over her milk. You clean up the spill while she continues to eat.	
5. You ask your child to help you put away groceries, but she keeps watching TV without responding. You keep calling her and continue to put groceries away.	

Answer key: 1. Attention 2. Accommodation 3. Antagonism
4. Acquisition 5. Avoidance

Now, in a notebook or journal, or just on a piece of paper, write down five of your child's most recent ADHD behaviors. Identify the situation in which the behavior occurred, and think of how your child profited. Is there one kind of reinforcement that seems to dominate your child's behavior?

Identifying Frequent Triggers

It's essential that you take a close look at your child's past experiences so that you can uncover what has reinforced her ADHD behavior over time. Consider why the consequences of ADHD behavior may be more reinforcing for your child than for others, given her history. There isn't one particular history that explains each kind of ADHD behavior, even though we do see patterns. Even very different histories can trigger and fuel ADHD behavior. For instance, a feeling of entitlement may contribute to a child's intrusiveness, but intrusiveness can also be learned by a child who would otherwise be left out or ignored. A child can show delayed self-management either with conscientious parents who take care of everything or with parents who are negligent, hasty, and disorganized. What issue or issues may be underlying your child's behavior?

There are a wide variety of possible factors in ADHD behavior. Three common ones are perceived insinuations of incompetence, a feeling of inferiority, and depleted parents.

Perceived Insinuations of Incompetence

A child may respond to a parent's checking and supervision as if this behavior insinuates the child is incompetent. The child might not recognize that the parent is anxious about safety and trying to be helpful. The child may wonder why the parent monitors and directs her actions so frequently. She may think that the parent is trying to control her or take away her opportunities to make decisions. She may accuse the parent of treating her like a baby.

In an attempt to prove the parent wrong, the child may take on more than she can handle and make more mistakes, which results in her parent hovering and directing her actions more. Her response to her parent makes the problem worse. As the cycle continues, she may become increasingly nonresponsive to feedback and more intense in her protest. Her quest to stop the parent increases the parent's attempts to stop her. ADHD behavior is stimulated in the process, and the pattern becomes the norm.

A Feeling of Inferiority

At other times, a child may see herself as inferior and incapable. She may feel that she is not as skilled as her sibling, who can outwit her during most arguments and outperform her. Her frustrations may build, and she may sidestep requirements so that she will not expose her incompetence. She may complain that her sibling gets all the positive attention, and she may view herself as a loser. Rather than try and possibly fail, she avoids competing with the star in the family, instead attracting attention with a variety of outlandish behaviors.

This does not mean that competent siblings cause ADHD. Many children with competent siblings do not show ADHD behavior. The point is that competent siblings can affect particular children in ways that increase ADHD behavior.

Depleted Parents

When a parent is not feeling well, a child's energy may be overwhelming. Any time a parent is emotionally depleted, that parent is likelier to withdraw, become irritable, or give in to a child's pestering to ease the situation quickly. If, for example, a parent stays in the bedroom until things get noisy, a child may learn a variety of ways to be loud and disruptive. Depleted parents can increase the probability of ADHD behavior because they more often respond in ways that reinforce it.

Although not all children will respond with ADHD behavior to a depleted parent, whenever there is impatience, distress, and lack of routine and follow-through, there is bound to be an effect on the way in which a child learns to self-manage and interact with others. ADHD behavior may work to the child's advantage by rendering the parent more powerless and provoking more attention. And it can be a way to avoid or antagonize someone who seems uncaring.

The Next Step

Now that you have some ideas about what triggers and fuels ADHD, and you're ready to learn effective ways of responding to diminish ADHD behavior and develop your child's self-reliance and cooperation. The next chapter presents the basic principles that you will use. These principles will guide you and help you maintain a pleasant relationship with your child, one involving give and take.

4 Ten Guiding Principles to Reduce ADHD Behavior

Your child must learn to function competently without you if he is going to succeed in life. He must learn skills to complete necessary tasks, and he must learn to understand other points of view so that his relationships may be positive. He must learn to balance what he wants with what others want without sacrificing his personal integrity. You can teach your child these things.

This chapter introduces you to ten principles that can help you decrease ADHD behavior and increase your child's self-reliance and cooperation. You can apply these principles when teaching your child basic self-care and when helping him interact with family members, peers, and teachers. These principles can help him manage effectively inside and outside of the home. They will help your child learn assertiveness without overstepping social boundaries. They will encourage him to seek assistance but not rely on you to do most of the work. And they will help him stay emotionally connected even though he is learning to solve problems on his own.

Principle 1: Use Coercion as a Last Resort

Most ADHD therapies recommend that you change your child's behavior by imposing a strict system of controls. Usual consequences will not be enough to protect him. You must step in and immediately entice him with extra rewards or punish him with restrictions. The thought is that only this kind of stringent parenting will keep him from the chaos that ADHD generates.

No doubt, disciplining in that fashion works quickly. It's easy to do, and all parents know that stringency is sometimes necessary to protect a child. Most agree, even when a parent wants to allow some decision making, it's often best to limit a child's options to a couple of acceptable alternatives (e.g., "We can play nicely, or we can put the game away"). Yes, coercion—disciplining with rewards and punishments—has a significant role in child rearing, but it has some downsides worth considering. Let's take a look at them; then we will look at an alternative strategy.

The Problems with Rewards and Punishments

When you manage your child's behavior using special incentives and penalties, things will seem fine as long as there is no controversy and your child keeps earning the rewards you control. He may even be happy that he is getting something extra for showing the behaviors that you expect. But this kind of coercion can be problematic when it's the primary way to socialize within a family, even though parents are often tempted to use this method of discipline to reduce their child's reliance on ADHD behavior.

For example, research shows that connecting a bribe to an activity will reduce a child's interest in doing the activity when the bribe is removed (Lepper, Greene, and Nisbett 1973). This research shows that once you introduce a reward system, you must keep using it to avoid a significant drop in performance. As long as you beat the drum, your child rows the boat, but if you stop, so does he.

When you are compelling your child with rewards and punishments, he may seem quite lazy when you are not pressing him to achieve. He conforms only if the bells and whistles are in effect, or he complies just long enough to get the pressure to stop. Often he does only the bare minimum. And he learns that he must be paid or punished just to behave acceptably.

Your child may also rush through whatever it takes to get to the designated prize and not "stop to smell the roses" along the way. So if you want your child to develop a variety of interests, you may be working against yourself and him when you use a reward system. Your discipline may increase your child's desire to obtain the reward and make the work seem worse than it is.

In addition, any reward system that you control is limited by the extent of your personal involvement. You want your child to be successful without you, but an invented system of rewards and punishments trains compliance only under supervision. You will not be able to monitor every action that your child takes, and so you will not have influence over him sometimes. Sadly, this will increasingly be the case as your child grows older and spends more time away from you. Moreover, he may find that, by lying and sneaking around, he can get away with doing what he wants when you cannot keep tabs on him. Even if you threaten to double the punishment for dishonesty, he may take that risk whenever he thinks he can "slip under the radar." A game of cat and mouse can develop whenever you socialize your child in this way.

But that is not all. What happens when your consequence is not strong enough to outweigh the hassle of meeting the expectation? For example, it's just not worth it to lug the trash outside when it's snowing just to get another star on the chart. Many children recognize this problem, and it's common for them to resist until the bribe or threat is increased.

This escalation is also apparent when you use "counting down" as a means of persuasion, as many parents find that their child waits until they reach the last number before they comply. Why move on "one" when you can wait until "three"? These children learn to procrastinate until the intimidation increases and makes it worthwhile to give up what they are doing. The relationship spirals into a power struggle, and they resist until enough pressure is applied.

As you can see, when your purpose is to create discomfort or give something extra to get your child to obey, you are teaching your child to overpower rather than to cooperate. He sees you trying to force submission, and he duplicates the same behavior to gain authority over you. You take away what he wants, so he takes away what you want. Even if it means putting himself in jeopardy, he may find a way to gain the upper hand. You pressure him to be more productive, and he learns ways to get you to reduce your expectations. You end up struggling for dominance. As he finds ways to outmaneuver you, you must find ways to close the loopholes. Empathy, attending to each other's perspective, scratching each other's back, and finding a middle ground are often set aside when you get into this arrangement.

Often relationships can deteriorate and become quite contentious. This can happen when your child tells you that there were good reasons for his failure to qualify for a prize. You then have two potential problems on your hands: you can be coldhearted and deny his plea for leniency, or you can risk giving in to what could be a lame excuse or outright lie. Neither choice is good. If you decide to go forward with the restriction, he may become resentful and think of ways to escape from your rule. You end up driving him away instead of bringing him closer. This is exactly what happens when we send people to jail. They spend much of their time trying to break free from, sidestep, and outsmart the people in charge, and the same problem will occur with your child.

There are plenty of negative side effects with coercive discipline. Your child may stop liking a reward so that you can no longer use it to pressure him. He may become overly concerned about unwanted consequences and develop anxiety. He may stop telling you what he likes so that you cannot withhold it to "pull his strings." Sometimes failure to obtain a privilege makes little difference to children as long as they remain in the center of their parents' concerns. And sometimes children don't want to let their parents win, no matter what the cost.

So ask yourself, *Does my child really need extra payment or the threat of a "time out" chair to be kind or honest?* Do you want him to agree to cooperate and help out only if he gets something extra in the deal, or do you want him to derive pleasure from building a caring relationship with you? Even if the reward is spending time together, do you really want to turn your time with each other into a business deal or make it an obligation? Of course not.

An Alternative

With all of these potential side effects, let's take a different approach. You can focus your child on the ultimate reason to cooperate and develop himself: he will have happier, more fruitful experiences if he is kind and skillful. There is no reason to distract him from this powerful motive. His social life and esteem will improve when he acquires new skills and cares for others. Nothing is more intoxicating than those outcomes; your child needs no other incentive. Isolation and lack of competence are the most potent negative consequences, and inclusion and knowledge are the most wanted treasures.

Your child can connect achievement and cooperation with something positive without your having to coax him with bribes or threats. Sometimes resolving the problems associated with a particular activity is all that it takes. Once that is accomplished, your child may learn to enjoy and complete a task without any additional compensation.

Even very young children can respond enthusiastically to a positive social reaction or accomplishment. Think of the immediate and profound influence that a mother's smile has on her infant. And think of your child's celebration the moment he solves a jigsaw puzzle.

Learning a New Language

You can get your child to behave well with less coercion, but first it's important that you learn how to speak with him in a less dominating fashion. Although it may seem simple to replace standard phrases with alternates, your habits of speech may be hard to break, especially when you're distracted or stressed. At first, you may trip over your words or not know what to say, but that is to be expected. Don't be discouraged, and give yourself a substantial opportunity to learn. It might help if in the beginning you choose to focus on changing just two or three phrases you use often. Each day, remind yourself about the changes you want to make. First, commit to catching yourself *after* speaking in the old way. Later on, you will catch yourself *while* you are speaking. With practice comes mastery, and you can expand your focus to include more of the list. Eventually, this new style of communication will become second nature for you.

Speaking Less Coercively (Ages 5–12)

Instead of using the words in bold print, try the alternatives. The change in language will help you develop a cooperative (rather than coercive) relationship with your child.

- **I'll let you** → I'd like it if you → It's fine for you to → It's not a problem for you to

- **Should** → Could

- **Must** → Might

- **It's a privilege** → It's an accommodation → It's a show of appreciation → It's special for you

- **This is your responsibility** → This is your opportunity → This is your contribution

- **I'm warning you** → I'm letting you know → I'm reminding you

- **You need to** → I'd like you to → It would be nice if you → It's safe to → It's a good idea to

- **I want you to** → It would be great if you

- **You have to** → I'd like it if you → It would be nice if you were willing to → It's important that you → Would you like to → You get to → Your job might be easier if you

- **Don't you like it?** → Do you like it?

- **I expect you** → I hope that you → I prefer that you

- **You have to** → You might → You could → It would help if you

- **You can't** → It could be a problem if you → It's probably better if you

- **You're not allowed to** → I don't want you to → It's too risky to → There's a safer way to

- **This is your chore** → Taking charge of this will help us → This could be your donation

- **I told you to** → I wanted you to

Principle 2: Stay Calm

Some professionals claim that "deficient emotional regulation" is a central feature of ADHD (Barkley 2009). For that reason it's imperative that you address this problem and help your child avoid extreme emotional states. One of the best ways to accomplish this is to model calm behavior for your child. When you model a behavior, you simply act in the same way you want your child to (a case of "Do as I do"), and your child learns by observation.

Children and grown-ups alike can be persuasive and intimidating when we overreact. Acting under the influence of excessive emotion can help us obtain what we want, help us get relief, or help us successfully defend ourselves. Even though there are side effects to behaving in this way, it can be difficult to stop. Often it will take a great deal of practice to break the habit of overreacting. But to be truly effective and have cooperative relationships, it's usually better to respond moderately.

Most people think and resolve problems more effectively when they are composed, so it's very important that you and your child understand life's events in less extreme ways. For example, if your child says, "You never let me…," you could say, "This time I'm saying no." If he says, "Stop yelling at me," you could say, "I must be sounding critical." If he says, "You always give *her* more," you can always say, "It's hard to keep things exactly the same. Maybe next time *you* will be the lucky one." Eliminating all-or-nothing thinking will help everyone stay calm and civil. Sometimes your child will get what he wants, and sometimes he will not, but over time, no one will be deprived.

You might also help your child understand the absurdity of his extreme responses by playfully exaggerating. For example, if he is having difficulty stopping a fun activity, such as reading a story, you could say in a joking tone, "Yes, we will never ever be able to read another story together again." Help him realize that a current disappointment does not mean permanent loss or total failure.

Your child's difficulties with self-control are not a permanent disability. In studies of children with self-control problems, some children did learn adequate self-control, and these children did not have health, financial, or social problems in adulthood (Moffitt et al. 2011).

Your child does not have to be a "hothead," and you can help him. For example, you could say, "I know you're disappointed that we couldn't play. What if you talked with me about your feelings instead of kicking the flowers?" Often the key is identifying *emotional triggers*: those unresolved problems, fears, and "old bruises" that a situation ignites. Let's say your mother-in-law has disrespected you in the past by not bothering to wipe her feet on the mat before she comes into your house. If one day your child neglects to wipe his feet and tracks mud into the house, you may feel just as disrespected. Even though the situation is different, you may react emotionally as though it were the same. To someone who did not know your history with your mother-in-law, your reaction (to your child) might seem irrational. Staying calm will often require that you identify your emotional triggers, and your child has emotional triggers too.

Tip

When your child is overreacting, do not escalate the problem. Keep your tone of voice calm and reasonable even if you are repeating yourself. The following responses can help curb hotheaded emotions:

- "I know you're angry, but I can hear you better if you talk quietly."

- "It's easier to work together if we're nice to each other and talk things out."

- "We can probably solve this better if we wait for you to calm down."

- "Will yelling change things?"

- "Is there a reason why you are so angry about this?"

- "Does yelling get me to say yes to you?"

As a last resort: Stop responding until your child settles himself. If necessary, create physical space between yourself and your child to facilitate "quieting down."

Increasing Serenity

When you are settled, consider the possible reasons for your overreacting at particular times. Maybe you tend to overreact if you keep encountering one problem after another that does not get resolved. Maybe you often let your discontentment simmer and then explode when you reach a boiling point. For example, if you feel as if you have bent over backward to please others all day long and yet as soon as you say the word "no," someone complains, you may overreact.

Sometimes, however, you may overreact because of things that happened in your first family many years ago. Current interactions may be reminding you of troublesome events in your childhood. But keep in mind, there are significant differences between then and now. There could be positive, less extreme ways to resolve your current dilemma. You might have options to solve current problems that were not available to you in the past. So take the time to figure out a comfortable resolution. That will help both you and your child stay calm and "emotionally regulated."

Actions That May Help You Stay Calm

It's important to know how to self-soothe. Your brain works better when you keep your composure. The next time you feel irritable, try one of the following suggestions and guide your child to do the same:

- Find a place to relax.

- Give yourself some time to decompress when you first come home from work or school.

- Slow down your breathing, relax your body, and think of something you enjoy.

- Wait twenty minutes before returning to a stressful situation.

- Distract yourself by doing an activity that you enjoy.

- Remind yourself that you will be less remorseful and more effective when you are calm.

- Take a moment to think about things in your life that are going well.

- Think of a more moderate way to understand what is happening. Give someone the benefit of the doubt.

- Imagine the desired outcome: think of what you want to happen.

- Resolve problems one at a time.

- Think of similar problems that you have solved.

- Exaggerate the problem to the point of ridiculousness; humor can lessen tension.

- Think of ways to make things better.

Note: sleeping and eating well, and regular exercise, will help you handle difficulties more effectively.

Principle 3: Take Steps to Address and Resolve Problems

Some may think that reducing coercion means letting your child do whatever he wants. That is not the case. Your child can learn to conform to expectations even when your management style is less forceful. For example, while you may have to segregate a child who keeps bothering others, often not responding can be more powerful than intimidation, especially if he is profiting from all of the attention.

Don't worry about letting your child fail when you control less. You are actively using discipline that has fewer negative side effects. You might be allowing some failures to occur that would stop more quickly with coercion, but you are not idle even when you are less forceful. You are methodically developing mature behavior that your child will continue when you are not there, and many of his failures may prove meaningful in his learning.

You are not trying to be your child's friend or ask him for permission when you reduce coercion. You are taking firm steps to stop greediness, jealousy, neglect, and exploitation. You are also welcoming his input, looking for his contribution, and considering whether he is comfortable with what is happening. In fact, many parents find that their child is more open and accommodating when they reduce coercion. They are empowered by the new relationship that forms with their child.

You are reducing pressure tactics but persuading in more subtle ways. For example, you might play "devil's advocate" so that your child talks to you more freely. You might playfully ask, "Why would you want to wear a watch and know that it's time to stop the game?" Your question makes light of the fact that he benefits when he does not know the time. He might then talk more comfortably with you about the pros and cons of coordinating your schedules because the interaction is nonthreatening.

Questions That May Help Your Child Problem Solve with You (Ages 6–12)

Instead of solving problems *for* your child, you can solve problems *with* your child. The following questions will help you activate your child's thinking and participation when it's necessary to resolve a problem.

- "How do you want to handle that problem?"

- "What do you want to do about that?"

- "What are your options (choices, priorities)?"

- "What will we do if the problem keeps happening?"

- "What could you do to take better care of yourself in that situation?"

- "Will that be an improvement for you?"

- "What is it that you don't like?"

- "What do you think the problem is?"

- "What do you suggest?"

- "Do you think we're trying to be mean to you when we say no?"

- "What changes can we make to solve this?"

- "What has worked for you in the past?"

- "What's bothering you?"

- "What are you saying no to?"

- "Are you happy with the way we're doing it?"

- "Would you like to make some changes?"

- "What's your vote?"

- "Do you want to work on this problem together?"

Six Active Steps that You Can Take to Help Your Child Address and Resolve Problems

You are not being permissive or negligent when you discipline with less coercion. You are conscientiously helping your child do the following:

1. Understand the side effects of ADHD behavior without criticism or blame.

2. Identify positive alternative actions and outcomes.

3. Explore the complications, harms, and obstacles that he is likely to run into.

4. Be aware of past successes in similar situations so he is confident to try.

5. Break down complex achievements into manageable steps.

6. Address and resolve incidents that disrupt your relationship with him.

Principle 4: Be Patient

It may take some time for this new way of parenting to show results. So don't expect your child to stop ADHD behavior right away. As the saying goes, "Rome wasn't built in a day." You may have to revisit a problem on many different occasions before progress is evident. Know ahead of time, the profits associated with ADHD behavior will not go away the first time you try something new. Think of all the New Year's resolutions that you have made.

Some people will say that your child's ADHD keeps him from changing, but most people usually need more than one trial to change any of their behaviors, especially when the behavior is a habit they have had for many years. Let's say you have kept your forks in a particular drawer for a long time. If you start keeping your forks in a different drawer, you may mistakenly go to the old drawer for a fork on several occasions before you get in the new habit. We get accustomed to ways of behaving that have worked for us in the past.

Remember, problems will not go away immediately; relapse is expected. You can have a productive discussion with your child, and he may still behave in the same old way. Unforeseen obstacles may occur, and unexpected circumstances can arise that throw off your plans.

Instead of giving up or resorting to coercion, stay on the path of finding a mutually agreeable solution to the problem. Maintain the view that, over time, positive discussions and new learning will eventually take hold. The positive alliance you establish with your child will eventually promote the results that you want (Martin, Garske, and Davis 2000).

Teaching the Benefits of Open Communication

When operating in this new way, it's often necessary to talk with your child. But what happens if he does not want to respond when you ask for his input? What do you do when he is distant and hard to reach? Does his reluctance make it impossible for you to eliminate his ADHD behavior with this new style of parenting?

The answer is no! It's common for a child diagnosed with ADHD to avoid and expect negativity and blame when others want to address problems. He is unlikely to participate in a frank discussion until he learns the benefits of sharing ideas and cooperating. This is your first obstacle to overcome.

Therapists face similar difficulties during counseling sessions. Clients are often defensive and reluctant to talk about certain subjects. They avoid even though avoidance is costly to them. However, with patience and understanding, many clients eventually learn to talk more freely. Your job is to do the very same thing. You love and care for your child, and it's important that he feel secure that you can resolve problems together.

If you notice that your child is reluctant to problem solve, you will have to eliminate obstacles that are holding him back. Here are some typical roadblocks that parents encounter when they try to get their child to openly communicate and work as a team.

- He likes it when you do the work to solve the problem.

- He is not ready to give you a response.

- He avoids accountability when he remains silent.

- He doubts that talking will lead to success.

- He wants you to leave him alone.

- He is too angry to cooperate with you.

- He likes things the way they are.

- He keeps expectations low.

- He knows you care when you press him to talk.

- His withholding gets you to make concessions.

The "I Don't Know" Syndrome

Perhaps your child is in the habit of saying "I don't know" when you ask for his input. In some instances, this may be a true statement. However, even when he could easily guess or make a suggestion, he may still claim absolute ignorance. When he responds in that way, it's safe for you to assume that he is avoiding or withholding. A child with ADHD is very adept at being elusive. He may hide under his jacket or hat, and you may often hear him say, "Maybe," "Kind of," "Sort of," "Yep," "I don't care," "What?" "Huh?" "I guess," "Sure," "What do you want me to say?" or "I have no clue" when you want him to talk with you about an issue. It can feel like pulling teeth to get him to connect. Often he halfheartedly shrugs or looks away and fidgets with a toy instead of gazing in your direction. This way of responding has probably been brewing for quite some time. He is hard to reach, and he maintains control over you when you beg him to respond or you keep repeating yourself.

So how do you build a secure relationship in which your child talks without reservation, sharing what he thinks and feels? This can be difficult after many disagreeable years and frequent reliance on you and others to solve problems. You may even notice that he talks more freely to strangers.

Breaking Down Barriers (Ages 6–12)

The "I don't know" syndrome is self-protective, and it may not break down immediately. But remain optimistic. You can eventually develop a style of interacting that makes it safe for your child to talk openly. He can eventually learn that positive changes can happen when you speak with each other. Here is a way to accomplish that goal.

- Find out whether your child is open to changing or whether he is content with keeping things the same.
    - Talk with him about the consequences of leaving the problem (e.g., leaving his bike on the front lawn) unresolved, without implying that he should change.
    - Is he prepared to deal with those consequences?
    - Does he want you to solve the problem without his input?
    - Is he comfortable giving you the message that he does not care?
- Often it helps to use humor or playful sarcasm to put him at ease. For example, you could say, "Of course we all like arguing in the car. It makes for a fun and safe trip. Let's not change a thing."
- Talk with your palms open rather than with your finger pointed.
- Positive tone is very important; it will help him open up.
- Make the problem seem less intimidating and overwhelming.
- Ask him to say whatever ideas come to mind without being concerned whether he is right or wrong.
- You may have to ask him the same questions in many different ways before you get a response. If he is not reacting, ask him, "What if you took a guess?"
- You are training assertiveness, so make it safe for him to be candid.
    - Ask him, "What's the worst thing that could happen if you told me what you think?"

- Reassure him that you will remain positive and reasonable, and encourage him to tell you when he is upset.

- Rather than lecture, create a volley. Try to develop a comfortable exchange.

  - Say your ideas simply and in as few words as possible.

  - Share the floor.

  - Allow him to initiate, engage, and express ideas.

- Let him know that his ideas are important. They can help determine family policy.

  - Demonstrate that you are willing to work hard to understand his point of view.

  - After he speaks, say back what you think he said. Then ask: "Did I get that right? Is there anything else you'd like to tell me?"

- Allow him time to speak and complete his ideas before jumping in.

- If you are unsure of what he is saying, encourage him to clarify. That will help you stay connected. Ask, "Would you make that easy for me to understand? I don't want to miss out on what you're saying."

- Check to make sure he is comfortable with what you are saying. Ask him: "How do you feel about doing it that way? Is this something that will work for you?"

- Notice when he is disengaging. Immediately address that problem. It's pointless to continue if he is dropping out. If he rolls his eyes, frowns, or looks away, or if he changes the subject or starts to fidget, find out what he does not like. Ask him:

  - "You don't look very excited. What are you feeling?"

  - "What gave you trouble?" (validate and empathize)

  - "What would be a better way to solve this?"

  - What can I do to make it easier for you to talk with me?"

Building a rapport. Creating a positive relationship with your child is essential. You want him to know that you are not the enemy when you guide the family and set limits. Most of the time, your policies and procedures benefit both of you. You are not denying him simply to promote yourself. When that is firmly established, he may give up the "I don't know" syndrome and work with you rather than against you.

Helping Your Child Understand Why (Ages 5–10)

Instead of giving your child a command, as on the left in the following table, try to give the same instruction in a less demanding way, as on the right. By explaining the reason for your direction you may find yourself needing to give commands less often, because your child understands why your direction is beneficial. You do not want to justify and explain every action that you take, but your child may become more cooperative and knowledgeable if you do not frequently tell him simply, "Because I said so!"

Commanding your child	Helping your child understand why
"Stop being so rough with that toy."	"If you're gentle, that toy will last longer."
"Get your drink yourself."	"If you get your own drink, you'll know how to do it and you won't have to wait for me."
"I want you to shut off the lights and go to sleep."	"The doctor says kids your age need eleven hours of sleep." "You'll feel better when it's time to get up in the morning if you shut the light off soon."
"You have to use your alarm clock."	"If you learn to use the alarm, you're free! You can be on time wherever you sleep." "It will help us get off to a good start together."
"Go wash up."	"Washing up will help you stay healthy and refresh you."

"I want you to pick up your things right now."	"If you pick up your things as soon as you're finished, you won't have to go back later."
"You have to write a thank-you note."	"If you show your appreciation, she'll be happy that she bought a gift for you."
"You have to pay attention."	"Your schoolwork will be easier to complete if you pay attention."
"I'm not going to stay here until you fall asleep."	"It's better for you to fall asleep without me so you can sleep well even when I'm not around."
"You're playing on the computer too much, so I'm limiting you."	"Life will be easier and more interesting if you develop many different kinds of skills."
"Answer me!"	"If I know how you feel, maybe we can work out something good for both of us."
"The rule is don't jump on the furniture."	"It's better if we spend our money on things that we like instead of having to buy another couch."
"You have to clean up after your friends."	"It's easier to have company at the house if I know you'll pick up when they leave."
"I want to hold your money."	"It might be easier to save for that expensive toy if you keep your money in a special place."
"You can't have food in your room."	"Let's keep the food in the kitchen so we won't get bugs where you sleep."
"Knock it off and take a bath now."	"You can play in the bath longer if you get in real soon."
"Put that down!"	"It's better to leave that alone. It breaks easily."
"Be quiet!"	"We can stay longer if we're quiet."
"Leave your iPod in the house."	"Your iPod will be safer if you keep it at home."
"Chew with your mouth closed."	"If we eat quietly, it's easier for us to talk and relax together. Would you be willing to help us out?"

Principle 5: Suspend Judgment

Evaluation can stimulate achievement and be helpful under some circumstances. But your child may relate to you more honestly and show more attentiveness if on occasion you suspend judgment and hear him out. You want your child to open up to you, and that will feel easier for your child when he is safe from criticism. Bickering about whose idea is right often spirals into a nonproductive interaction that leaves you at odds. Rather than resolve the problem, you spend most of your time in one-upmanship. Instead of listening, you concentrate only on what you want to say.

If your child twitches and pulls away (e.g., saying "Stop staring at me"), this may relate to uneasiness about correction, so noncritical interacting may help settle him down physically as well. You can put him at ease and make it comfortable for him to speak his mind by talking with him in a frank and respectful manner. Impartial statements about observations and facts will make it easier to resolve problems and build a relationship that both of you can value and enjoy. For example, if he complains, "You don't care about me," you can ask, "What gets you to feel that way?" This will help you identify the underlying source of the problem a lot better than insisting that he is wrong.

Developing a Welcoming Relationship (Ages 5–12)

You can learn to suspend judgment and speak in a manner that makes it easier for your child to share what he is thinking and feeling. Instead of making evaluative statements, as on the left in the table below, try more welcoming alternatives, as on the right.

Evaluative statement	More welcoming alternative
"This report card is terrible. It makes me look like a bad parent."	"How do you feel about this report card? What do you like about it? Is there anything you want to change?"
"You did a good job reading."	"It looks like you really enjoyed reading that story."

"You missed a spot."	"Thank you; it was nice of you to do that. Would you mind cleaning over here as well?"
"Be a good boy in school."	"Have a nice day."
"I need to check your work."	"Are you all set, or would you like another pair of eyes to take a look?"
"This one is wrong."	"How do you want to handle it if I find a problem?" "Would you like to look at this one again?"
"I'm proud of you."	"Congratulations!" (give a hug) "I'm happy for you." "Is it the way you imagined?" "Let's celebrate!" "It's spectacular." "You really know how to work hard and achieve." "How did you do that?" "Look what you did all by yourself."
"You behaved better this week."	"It was nice being together this week."
"You'd better learn to do it right."	"Would you like to practice and learn the skill?"
"Good job!"	"Thank you."

Principle 6: Say It Positively

If you are using a lot of negative language, switching to to positive language will help your child learn the advantages of behaving acceptably. Positive language can reduce anxiety, increase participation, and minimize ADHD behavior. Your child will also learn to think positively when the language that he learns and uses is affirming.

Putting things in negative terms can steer your child in that direction and, unfortunately, increase the behavior you want to stop. For example, telling your child not to think of pink elephants may only get him to think about pink elephants more. Saying that money burns a hole in his pocket or that he has problems just like his father may only increase those behaviors. While it's important that your child be aware of negative consequences and comply immediately when you tell him not to do something, too much emphasis on the negative can be counterproductive.

Exercise: Translate the Negative into the Positive (Ages 5–12)

Below are seventeen statements with a negative focus. Each is followed by an example of a positive alternative statement—but don't look yet. Use a piece of paper to cover the statements, then move it down until you can read the first negative statement. Try to think of a positive way to motivate your child's acceptable behavior without using words like "don't," "can't," and "stop." Then slide the paper down until you can see the positive alternative. With practice, positive language will become natural and automatic.

Negative: "If you don't let me finish my shopping, you won't get your allowance."

Positive: *"Instead of having to come back to finish our shopping, we can finish now and have time to play later."*

Negative: "You're wasting time again."

Positive: *"Maybe it will work out better for you if you start that project now rather than later."*

Negative: "Don't bother me right now."

Positive: *"I can play in a little while."*

Negative: "Don't be late for supper."

Positive: *"We look forward to eating with you at five thirty."*

Negative: "You can't have snacks before dinner."

Positive: *"Let's keep our appetites. We can eat together real soon."*

Negative: "If you don't do your work, you're going to fail."

Positive: *"If you complete your work, you might enjoy what happens."*

Negative: "Why are you touching those things on my desk!"

Positive: *"Would you please play with these toys over here instead?"*

Negative: "You can't play video games before school because you don't get ready on time."

Positive: *"Let's think of a way for you to play the game and still be ready to leave on time."*

Negative: "You always make a mess on the floor when you go to the bathroom."

Positive: *"I know you're a good aim. Maybe you could do that in the bathroom."*

Negative: "You're always making me wait for you."

Positive: *"I like it when you're on time."*

Negative: "If you can't keep up, you'll have to get a tutor."

Positive: *"We're willing to set aside money to get a tutor for you."*

Negative: "If you keep poking me, you can't sit on my lap."

Positive: *"How about we relax together and cuddle?"*

Negative: "You can't get it because it's too expensive."

Positive: *"Maybe we can afford it if we save and you pitch in some of your own money."*

Negative: "I don't trust you to have a house key."

Positive: *"I'll feel comfortable giving you a key when I know you're careful with your belongings."*

Negative: *"Don't interrupt."*

Positive: *"I'm almost finished."*

Negative: *"Don't take the last one."*

Positive: *"Do you mind sharing the last piece?"*

Negative: *"Stop dragging. We can't be late for our appointment."*

Positive: *"Let's get going. After we get there we can take it easy."*

Principle 7: Treat Your Child as Competent to Succeed

Your child will improve more quickly when you treat him as competent to succeed (Rosenthal 1987). Before assuming that he is inept, assess his competency when he is doing something he really enjoys or when he is doing tasks that he has practiced (e.g., playing Pokémon). Use those activities to gauge what he can do under positive circumstances. Maybe he is more capable than you think.

Let your child know that he is impressive, and allow him to teach and inform you. This will put him in the driver's seat, and it will reassure him that he can take the lead and do well on his own. Value his achievements and contributions, and take notice of his ingenuity and his ambition even if these traits show only with his hobbies. Your positive responses will help him repeat similar behaviors with other activities in the future.

Respecting Your Child's Competence (Ages 5–12)

When you treat your child as competent, you encourage achievement. Instead of making statements that imply a lack of competence, as on the left in the table that follows, try to communicate confidence in your child's ability to succeed, as on the right.

The child is unable	The child is competent
"Do you remember that we have an agreement?"	"Do we still have an agreement?"
"I'm going to set a timer."	"Would a timer help?"
"I want you to study for a least a half hour."	"How much preparation do you want before you take the test?"
"You need consequences for those poor grades."	"How important is school to you?" "What kind of grades would you like to have?"
"Let me help you."	"I'm available if you'd like to talk things over."
"I'm going to lock this up so you won't touch it."	"Can I count on you to leave this alone?" "Will you wait until we can do this together?"
"I made a list of what you have to do after school."	"Would making a list make it easier for you to get things done after school?"
"You have to read the directions."	"How can you find out what to do?"
"You're not allowed to play with those toys because you didn't pick them up yesterday."	"After you finish playing, are you okay with picking up when it's time to stop?"
"I'm waiting here to make sure you do it."	"Will you do it very soon?"
"Put your shoes in the cabinet and put your pants in the drawer."	"Where do you want to put your pants and shoes?"
"Can you put that away?"	"Will you put that away?"
"I don't trust you. You have to earn it."	"Would you like to take good care of each other?"
"You can't keep the crumbs off the floor."	"It doesn't seem as if you've been eating carefully."

Principle 8: Establish "Buy In"

When your child is comfortable with what is happening, he is more likely to cooperate and do his part. Everyone agrees that ADHD behavior decreases when there is interest (i.e., something the child wants to do, not something he has to do). For this important reason, it's good practice to obtain "buy in" when you are trying to get him to accommodate. Look to see whether he nods his head, smiles, or says "Okay" in a sincere fashion. And pay attention to whether he does the plan on his own before assuming that he is genuinely contented with it.

For many years, businesses have recognized that workers' productivity increases when they have input into how the company operates. Your child is also more likely to contribute and work hard when he has a say in family policy. His interest in doing what you want will increase when he knows that you are concerned about his preferences. For example, when figuring out when it's best for him to do a job, you might say, "If you start right after school, are you sure you will have enough time to play before it gets dark?" Your acknowledgement of his point of view reassures him that his feelings are important and that you are not just interested in getting work completed.

Remember, if you pressure your child, or if he suspects that you're trying too hard to convince him, he may believe that you are pushing him into what you prefer. His "buy in" will be weak. He may say what you want to hear just to get you to leave him alone. He may not have the slightest intention of following through, and he may regret any concessions that he made.

Conversely, when you act with concern about your child's perspective, you model responses that will benefit him throughout his life. Research shows that when infants and caretakers resolve problematic interactions by adjusting to each other in positive ways, their relationships become stronger. The child develops trust and security with the caretaker, his self-regulation improves, and the positive attachment builds a foundation that helps to protect him from future psychological problems (Sroufe 2005).

Being Proactive Can Help

If you know that a situation is likely to negate your child's point of view and perhaps trigger an ADHD behavior, you can take preventive action. For example, you might let your child know that you will be busy preparing a meal very soon. You might ask him whether he wants to join you or whether he would like to do something else while you're busy. Your thoughtfulness and interest in making sure he is comfortable with what will happen next reassures him that you care. This is a great way to increase cooperation and decrease ADHD behavior.

Establishing "Buy In" (Ages 5–12)

One way to increase your child's buy in is to allow him to direct the interaction. The recommendations below will help you establish strong buy in from your child. If you like, make a recording of your attempt to solve a problem, then watch or listen to it and evaluate how accurately you followed these recommendations. The goal is to figure out a mutually agreeable solution.

- Find out what your child wants to do to solve the problem. Hold back from offering solutions. Treat him as capable of working on a solution.

- Give him time to break silences. React to him rather than have him react to you. If there is a long pause, ask him what he is thinking about.

- Treat him as the expert.

  - Ask questions that explore his ideas.

  - Ask questions if you think there may be a problem with his solution (e.g., "What might happen if we take your friend with us without telling his parents?").

  - If you have an idea, find out whether he likes it (e.g., "What if you put the trash can out the night before?").

- Check to see whether he is satisfied with the solution.

Principle 9: Assert Yourself

A frequent problem for couples is the tendency of each person to blame the other for difficulties and demand that the other person change. In an ideal world, you would not have to change in response to difficulties—others would accept the blame and do the changing. But things do not work out like that very often. Waiting for others to behave differently may mean waiting forever.

A similar problem may occur with your child. You may tell your child what you want him to do, but if he resists or disregards you, his lack of cooperation may keep you stuck. However, instead of remaining frustrated, you can take the reins. You can assert yourself, and your child must then deal with the changes you have made. You do not have to be powerless. When you act first to solve a problem, you can get things moving.

So don't confuse less coercion with weakness or inactivity. If your child ignores you, rather than repeat the same instruction, you can take assertive action and physically stop him from what he is doing, without saying a word. There is no point repeating what he already knows. If he does not shut off the TV when it's time to do so, you can casually walk over and shut it off yourself. If he says, "I'll do it later," you can always let him know, "It's important to do it now."

Asserting yourself will mean talking with your child about problems more often, beginning with a focus on you and what you are willing and not willing to do. Let your child know you value his input, but don't stand still and let him control what happens; feel free to say "no thank you" and state your boundaries. As Kathryn Kvols (1998) advises, be both kind and firm.

Asserting Yourself (Ages 5–12)

Instead of asking your child to make a change, as on the left in the table that follows, focus on your own actions, as on the right. When resolving a problem, focus on what you can do to improve the situation and inform your child. Tone is important: assertiveness works better when delivered kindly.

Asking your child to make a change	Asserting yourself
"You'll have to make your own breakfast tomorrow because I have a meeting."	"It won't work out for me to cook breakfast for you tomorrow. Will that be a problem?"
"You're not allowed to eat all of the snacks."	"I'm happy to keep buying these snacks if we figure out a way to share them."
"Don't forget to let me know what we're doing."	"We can make plans if you let me know before three o'clock."
"Hurry up! We need to get you to school!"	"I'm going out to the car. What will you tell your teacher if you're late?"
"Pick up the toys on the floor."	"I'll be happy to come into your room when the toys are off the floor and I won't trip."

Principle 10: Foster Independence

You want your child to succeed, and you know that you will not always be around to protect him. You can enhance his survival and welfare when you help him learn self-reliance. However, this can be difficult when you are anxious about harmful consequences, and as you know, children with ADHD are not shy about getting into jeopardy.

Coming to your child's rescue and protecting him are necessary whenever you sense significant danger. However, you can make changes that help your child manage his affairs more competently on his own. You might even find that he learns many valuable lessons when you allow "natural consequences" to run their course.

Three Ways to Develop Your Child's Autonomy (All Ages)

These three recommendations will help you foster your child's independence, self-management, and persistence as he makes his way in the world.

1. Let your child experience the natural results of his actions, if there can be no significant harm (e.g., don't retrieve a toy that he has forgotten until it's convenient to do so).

2. Give your child an opportunity to solve problems on his own before offering assistance (e.g., let him struggle a little before helping him untie his shoelace).

3. Ask questions before giving answers, if you think he has a chance for success (e.g., "Why do you think it's better to ask me before your friend arrives if he can stay for dinner?").

Exercise: Increase Your Child's Self-Reliance for Five Different Tasks (All Ages)

Think of five things that you currently do for your child that he could probably successfully do on his own instead of relying on you. For example, instead of ordering for him at a restaurant, encourage him to order his own meal. Write your ideas in a journal or notebook or just on a piece of paper. If you are having trouble, think of some things that other children his age can do independently—your child can probably do many of these things as well.

Now encourage your child to attempt these tasks on his own, offering only enough help to keep things moving forward. If necessary, give a demonstration, and see whether he can imitate the basic steps. Resist the urge to take over or to correct your child when he does an imperfect job; it's okay if he makes a mistake.

The Next Step

Remember the ten guiding principles to reduce ADHD behavior:

1. Use coercion as a last resort.

2. Stay calm.

3. Take steps to address and resolve problems.

4. Be patient.

5. Suspend judgment.

6. Say it positively.

7. Treat your child as competent to succeed.

8. Establish "buy in."

9. Assert yourself.

10. Foster independence.

In the next chapter, you will begin to apply these principles to your situation. A good place to start is the development of your child's self-care. That is the most basic kind of self-management. Your child is no longer a toddler, and his mastery of self-care will make life significantly easier for both of you.

5

Teaching Your Child Self-Care

Now let's put the principles from the previous chapter to work. Our starting place is developing your child's self-care. Of course, you will provide support whenever necessary, but your child will have an advantage if she learns to manage her self-care independently. Because she will be more likely to follow through if she is eager to be self-reliant, the strategies in this chapter are designed to promote her enthusiasm.

When developing independence, it's preferable if your child learns to carry out self-care in response to cues in her environment rather than relying on your verbal guidance. For example, teach her to wake up to an alarm clock rather than your voice. Also, remember to treat your child as competent to succeed (principle 7): assume that she can learn to put toothpaste on her own toothbrush, pour her own glass of milk, use a watch, select her own clothes, and dress on her own. According to Jane Nelsen (1987), even very young children can master these kinds of tasks, and you can expect the same with your child.

Your child may have a history of not showing age-appropriate responsibility. According to research, children diagnosed with ADHD are on average 30 percent behind other children in their self-management skills (Pfiffner and Barkley 1998). Unless you tell your child to wash after using the bathroom, pick up after herself, brush her teeth, unzip her jacket, and so on, she may not do these things and accomplish little in the way of self-care. But why is she not learning routines and habits that seem so simple?

Emphasizing the Advantages

When you attempt to teach your child self-care, she may respond to your efforts in a negative fashion. She may feel as if you are pulling away, making her do more work, and taking away your attention and companionship. When that happens, she may balk at doing the self-care that you know is important.

Much as with weaning, many children feel pushed away by parental attempts to promote their self-care. They are reluctant to give up the assistance that parents offer, and they are apprehensive about abandonment when their parents are not involved in every detail of their lives. They may fear that any self-sustaining behavior would allow their parents to focus on other concerns (including their siblings).

If you suspect this is the case, ask your child the rhetorical question, "Do you think I'd forget about you if you took better care of yourself?" Also say, "I wonder whether you'd enjoy being more grown up with me," and imagine what you could do together.

Help your child recognize the advantages of self-reliance. For example, she can go more places without you, others will not harp on her so frequently, and she can accomplish tasks when help is not available. You want her to know that she will gain more than she loses when she demonstrates responsible self-care. The language that you use and your tone of voice can influence whether she responds positively, and it always helps to notice her developing self-care and willingness to help others.

Highlighting the Advantages (Ages 5–12)

Your child might be more interested in doing self-care when you focus on the benefits. Here are some examples of how to go from demanding that your child do self-care to pointing out the advantages.

Demanding self-care	Pointing out the advantages to self-care
"You'd better not lose those gloves."	"If you take good care of those warm gloves, you'll have them when it's cold."

"I hope you are going to put your watch on the bureau because you're always losing it."	"After you learn to keep your watch safe, we'll figure out a way to get you a better one."
"You have to clean your room."	"I wonder whether it'll be easier to find things if they're in special places, off the floor." "If you do the cleaning, you can put things where you like them."
"Go back and make your bed."	"If you make your bed, it might be more comfortable for you to get into later." "It would be a nice favor if you made your bed and helped neaten up the house."
"You can't go out to play now because we're leaving soon."	"You can go out because I know you'll come back on time."
"Now that you're in kindergarten, you'll have to do it on your own."	"Now that you're in kindergarten, you can show me how to do it."

Helping Your Child Follow Through Independently

It's important to help your child do what she says she will do without having to remind her. Researchers have developed a way to help people follow through with their intentions (Gollwitzer 1999). When you help your child "plan for success" in this special way, there is an increased chance that she will *instantaneously* carry out her plan on her own.

Ask your child to tell you what she wants to do and define when, where, and how she will do it, similar to if she were rehearsing for a play. Then have her identify the signals in the environment that will remind her to carry out her plan. Having her rely on the environment to cue her allows you to step aside. Because she takes the lead, her commitment to follow through is likely to be stronger as well (remember principle 10: foster independence).

The effects of this approach can be remarkable. For example, if your child wants to remember to bring back a library book at the end of the week, she can decide to put the book near her musical instrument that she always brings to school for Friday band practice. This will allow her to see the book before she leaves the house on that day, which will signal her to return it.

Example: Helping Your Child Remember Her Backpack for School (Ages 6–12)

Nine-year-old Sonia keeps forgetting to bring her backpack with her when she leaves the house in the morning. Her mother, Maria, helps her learn to follow through independently.

Maria: Looks like you've been forgetting to take your backpack to school. Has that been a problem for you?

Sonia: Yes. I need it for my lunch and homework.

Maria: Would you like to figure out a way to remember it?

Sonia: Yes.

Maria: Okay. Let's work out the details. Is there something that you always take with you in the morning?

Sonia: My bracelet.

Maria: How do you remember to take your bracelet?

Sonia: I always keep it on my bureau. I see it when I'm getting dressed.

Maria: Would it help if you could see your backpack in the morning, just like your bracelet?

Sonia: Yeah. Hey, I could put it next to my bureau.

Maria: Would that help you remember to take it with you?

Sonia: Well, I'd see it, but I put my bracelet on as soon as I get dressed, and I don't leave until later. I might still forget it if it's in my room.

Maria: So where do you want to put it so that you'll always see it and remember it before you leave?

Sonia: If I leave it next to the door, I'll always see it.

Maria: What will help you remember to put it next to the door each night?

Sonia: *(after a moment)* When I finish my homework in the evening, I'll put it near the door.

Maria: What might help you remember to do that?

Sonia: When I finish my homework, I always put it in my backpack. I can put my backpack next to the door when I finish my homework.

Maria: Is the extra time and effort worth it?

Sonia: Yup.

Maria: Would you like to have a place near the door that is special for your backpack?

Sonia: Sure.

Maria: What else can you do to make sure you bring the backpack into school?

Sonia: Let's see…when I get in the car, I can keep it between my legs.

Poor Hygiene

You can constantly remind your child to brush or wash, but that might not be the best solution for you. Also, if your child depends on your efforts, she will not learn to manage on her own in this regard. She may also dislike the constant reminding and think that you doubt her competence.

Your child knows that you agonize over her hygiene, and her failure to meet your standards could become a powerful weapon to punish you when she is angry (see "Antagonism," in chapter 3). Moreover, if she likes the fact that you worry about her, she may be reluctant to give that up as well. Often children are reassured that their parents care about them when they overreact to hygiene failures.

There can be many different reasons for a child's failure to carry out the simple routines of self-care. Here are a few examples.

- Robert was influenced by poor modeling; he was copying the lackluster way his parents maintained their hygiene.

- Fine motor problems interfered with Michael's self-care; he struggled more than others do, and his parents got into the habit of doing self-care for him.

- Philip felt safer when his body odor kept others at arm's length.

It's vital that you identify what hampers your child in this area. Thankfully, it's not always the case that children see hygiene in a negative light. For example, children are often reluctant to get out of the shower once they get in. Their unwillingness to start a hygiene-related task seems to have very little to do with the activity being unpleasant.

Solutions

Negative language and coercion can often have a detrimental effect on your child's response to hygiene, and that is often a factor when there is resistance. Checking to see whether she used soap when she washed her hands, or forcing her to apply it, will only make hand washing an unhappy experience that she will resent. When you sense a power struggle around washing her hands, you could ask her instead: "What's going on? Are you okay with letting germs live on your hands, or are you unhappy because you feel that I'm ordering you around?" Staying positive, keeping the enjoyment, and complimenting your child's expertise will encourage her cleanliness.

Now let's focus on brushing teeth as an example. You can ask your child if she would like to take care of her teeth and find out when she would like to brush them. If she wants a suggestion, you could say, "The dentist says to brush them after each meal. This will keep your teeth healthy and strong" (principle 6: say it positively).

Avoid perpetuating your child's dependency. Rather than brush your child's teeth, show her how to do it. Say, "I can show you how the dentist taught me" (principle 7: treat your child as competent to succeed). Help her recognize that she is taking good care of herself when she manages her hygiene. Healthy teeth need less repair work (which is never very pleasant), and your child may like it when others notice her healthy smile and remark about how nice she looks.

Sometimes, however, your child may be testing to see whether she has the right to say no to a hygiene request, and you might acknowledge that problem rather than always insist. The world will not end if her hygiene is poor for a brief time. Your child might be less resistant if you do not always apply pressure (principle 4: be patient). As the saying goes, "Pick your battles." Your child's poor hygiene may have little to do with not understanding the consequences of her actions. As you know, many people do all kinds of things to themselves to prove a point.

If the problem persists, you can get things going by doing a reality check. You want your child to be clear about what could happen if she continues to be negligent. For example, when Nick kept forgetting to use his orthodontic "appliance," it was important to remind him that his failure could result in significant jaw malformation. His mother asked, "Is not wearing it worth that much to you?"

When your back is against the wall, you can always raise the question, "Would you be willing to do it even though you don't want to?" After all, most of us do things that we do not want to do. Responsible self-care, like most socially valued behavior, requires adherence to schedules and other limits whether we like it or not. We all confront that inconvenience, and we learn to comply even when we are not head over heels. Assume that your child can learn to do the same.

Developing Routines

It's important to develop consistent routines for things like washing your hands and body and brushing your teeth. That is how most people ensure adequate hygiene. Similar to our example of Maria helping Sonia with her backpack, try to help your child identify environmental signals that will remind her to brush and wash. For example, the invitation to start a meal could signal her to wash her hands. Getting into her pajamas could signal her to brush her teeth. As always, the goal is to develop a routine that she can do without you.

If your child is not doing her routine, instead of spelling out each step, you might say, "It's getting late" or "We have to leave soon." This will give her greater opportunity to self-manage as compared with telling her exactly what to do. If you notice that she has omitted a step in her bedtime routine—brushing her teeth—you could ask, "Is there anything else that you still might like to do before you go to sleep?" Only as a last resort, you might ask, "Are you sure you want to go to bed without brushing?"

Being Firm

It does not make sense to force a child to do hygiene unless there is no other option, and this will work only when she is very young and easy to overpower physically. But firm limits can increase your child's willingness to accommodate. For example, if she continues to neglect her teeth, you might say, "We may have to use some of our movie money to pay for extra trips to the dentist." Because her lack of self-care also leaves her susceptible to cavities, you might add, "You can continue to not brush, but in that case it's probably best that I don't buy the snacks that can be bad for your teeth" (principle 9: assert yourself).

You are not trying to make your child suffer; you are protecting, not punishing, her. You are resolving a dilemma assertively and taking firm action whether or not it bothers her. Your solution helps her understand how her negligence affects others as well as herself.

Ostracizing

In some extreme circumstances, you may find it necessary to ostracize your child to solve her lack of hygiene. Because it's important to be considerate of others, you might say, "We would love to have you join us, but only if you're willing to wash and get dressed in clean clothes." If she continues to resist, you might ask her: "Is there a reason to create this kind of problem for the family? Is something else bothering you?"

If there is no progress, and if it's feasible to have someone stay home with her, you could leave your child behind when you go out. If you have to pay someone to monitor her, you can talk about how that will affect the family budget. If you want her to bear the cost more directly, you can require her pay the sitter with her personal money (or sell a few of her toys if she does not have cash). Yes, she has the power to sabotage, but she also misses out on the excursion and helps offset the inconvenience with her personal funds. She then decides whether it's worthwhile to neglect hygiene.

Difficulties with Dress

Your child likely shows problems with dressing, buttoning, and zipping (Roizen et al. 1994), so it's important that she practice those skills. Unfortunately, she may not be enthusiastic about giving up your help. She may, for example, call out "Ma!" and then nonchalantly lift her leg and wait for you to put on her sock (see "Accommodation," in chapter 3). You may feel negligent if you do not assist her, but don't reinforce laziness or entitlement by offering that kind of aid.

Instead, give only enough assistance to maintain steady progress. If you offer help as soon as your child complains or says, "I can't," her self-care skills will falter. Asking her to clarify what she can't do is a positive first step that keeps the ball in her court.

Solutions

Helping your child develop self-help skills takes time. If you are rushed and pressured to get things done, you will not have the luxury of waiting for her to resolve difficulties and improve. She may doubt that she can learn quickly enough to meet expectations, and she may become disrupted and discouraged. If you plan, you can avoid this problem and things may work out better. For example, you can consider clothing options the night before, when there is time to work together. This beats getting frantic in the morning when time is short.

If your child has more authority with her clothes, she may also show more interest and cooperation. Rather than tell her what to wear on a cold day, you might simply point out, "It's cold outside." This will help her feel that she has more control over selecting her outfit. As she grows older, she can learn to check the weather herself.

Clothing Decisions

Sometimes you may have to insist on certain clothing to protect your child from the elements or to ensure that her outfit is appropriate. But often her clothing decisions will not be inappropriate enough to warrant coercive action. As your child's pediatrician will tell you, your child will not catch a cold just because she is underdressed—she will simply be cold. And if she is cold enough, she will likely make different choices in the future. That is the power of natural consequences.

On some occasions, you might be concerned that your child will spoil a family outing if she does not wear certain clothing. You may fear that she will become uncomfortable and make things miserable for others when you cannot turn back. In these situations, you could encourage her to bring certain articles along "just in case." Finding a convenient way to carry the extra clothing (so that she does not feel burdened) may also help. Remember, establish "buy in" (principle 8). Rather than force a solution, find an arrangement that is acceptable to both of you (principle 1: use coercion as a last resort).

When it's important that your child dress a certain way, let her know. For example: "These are the kinds of clothes we all wear to church. Which do you want to wear today?" Sometimes there are very few options. If your child continues to fuss, there may be other reasons for her reluctance to accommodate. As with hygiene, it's not always a clothing issue, so find out whether something else is bothering her. That may resolve the problem just fine.

But giving your child a say does not mean that she gets her way. For example, if you bring home clothes you have purchased for her and she does not want to try them on, let her know, "I can wait till tomorrow, but then I'll have to return them to the store." This kind of ordinary consequence may pique her interest and get her to check out the new clothes more quickly. If you continue to have difficulties with clothing purchases, shop for clothes for her only when she is with you.

Wearing the same outfit. You may also experience problems when your child wants to wear the same outfit too many days in a row. You might be concerned that you are being negligent when you allow this to happen, and you may worry about her grubby appearance and how others will respond.

While your child's attachment to her outfit might cause you some anxiety, ask yourself, *Is it really so terrible if she looks disheveled? Is it really worth quibbling about?* If the answer is yes, you might say to her: "I know that you really like those pants and that shirt. Maybe I can wash the shirt so it'll last longer. After the shirt is clean, I can wash the pants for you." With this approach, your child always keeps half of the outfit during the cleaning process.

You may think that your child will continue to wear dirty clothes unless you force the issue, but negativity and rigidity are more likely when you are in a power struggle. So it's helpful to neither ridicule her nor wash her clothes when she has asked you not to. A mutually agreeable solution is usually better.

Compliments help. A great way to encourage competent dressing is to compliment your child when she looks exceptionally dapper. If she is not picking acceptable outfits or color combinations, instead of criticizing or joking about her crazy outfits (which may encourage silliness), notice when she is well coordinated. You might say: "Wow! You look sharp. You really know how to match those colors."

Exercise: Dressing Role Reversal (Ages 6–9)

If your child agrees, have her help *you* figure out what to wear. Putting her in the position of competence will help her develop mastery of the skills you want her to learn. Follow these steps:

- *First, ask her about the weather (provide help if she does not know how to get the forecast). This will help her narrow down your choices of outfits.*

- *Next, talk about where you will be going this day. It's her job to figure out what constitutes appropriate attire.*

- *Have her identify clothing combinations that work well together. Show excitement when she accurately matches colors.*

- *Finally, ask her to help you with your zippers and buttons. This will help her feel more confident that she has the skills to dress herself.*

Difficulties with Sleep

Sleep is essential to your child's health, so it's important to develop a good sleep routine. Getting up at the same time each morning (with no naps during the day) can help your child get into a natural twenty-four-hour cycle called a circadian rhythm. Variations in sleep routine on the weekend can make it difficult for your child to get up for school on Monday morning, so try to maintain some consistency. When your child has good sleep habits, she will eventually learn to wake at the same time each day even without an alarm.

Children diagnosed with ADHD frequently have sleep problems. They show more episodes of sleepiness during the day (Lecendreux et al. 2000), and their lack of sleep increases their behavior problems and inattentiveness at school (Aronen et al. 2000). That is why it's very important to find out what may be disrupting your child's sleep. See the following examples.

- Britney reacted to the requirement to go to sleep as an attempt to keep her from having fun. She heard her parents talking about "finally having free time to relax," and she wanted that as well. She felt deprived when forced to go to bed, and she resisted.

- Joey liked the undivided attention that he received from his parents in the evening. His reluctance to go to sleep extended his contact with them.

- Aden did not want to face school the next day. No alarm that his parents bought him was loud enough to get him out of bed. On school days, he was always tired and dragging.

- Rachel often heard arguing at night. Instead of relaxing, she lay awake fretting and as a result was sleepy the next day.

Identifying and resolving any problems that influence your child's sleep is essential. Often a child will resist sleep in the same way she resists all the other limits that you impose. If you say, "You have to sleep," she automatically asks, "Why?" and finds a reason to say no. Sometimes her reluctance is simply a ploy to get you to engage with her. Her failure to do the bedtime routine forces you to drop what you are doing, step into a drama, and worry about her well-being.

Solutions

If you have read Richard Ferber's (1985) sleep intervention, you know how important it is to have your child learn to sleep without depending on you. In many ways, the approach you are learning in this book is an extension of the Ferber method for many of the problems that you face with your child. You are teaching your child to manage life without your constant aid and relief (principle 10: foster independence).

The first step is to establish a nightly routine that your child can start and finish without you. From the beginning, try to establish a predictable time for starting the bedtime routine. You want her to stop doing other activities, perform hygiene, and get into her pajamas so that you can spend some time relaxing, reading, storytelling, and so on.

At first, you might provide a reminder, but pair it with other signals as soon as possible (a clock, the completion of a TV show, etc.). You might say, "Let's get ready for stories as soon as your show is over," but very quickly, you want your child responding to cues that occur without your involvement.

If your child ignores the routine you have developed, let her know that you are ready and waiting for her to start the bedtime activities. Mention that you will have more time together if she gets moving. This communicates that you are interested in sharing the special time that has been set aside.

Maintain Limits

While showing willingness to resolve any obstacles and being flexible when there are extenuating circumstances, you want your child to realize that bedtime has a firm beginning and end. Your child should know that when the clock strikes a certain hour, you are finished. Starting late means that both of you will have less special time together. If your child ignores the bedtime routine altogether, you may have to escort her to her room under duress. Setting firm limits will help her develop punctuality.

If your child comes out of her room when bedtime is over, don't cater to her. Neither is it advisable to punish her with another consequence, such as taking away TV or making bedtime earlier. Simply redirect her to her room without speaking (principle 2: stay calm). You can always ask her later on, "What can we do to make it easier to end your bedtime?" or "How do you want your bedtime to end?" to help resolve the problem.

Explore obstacles. A flawless bedtime routine may be difficult to achieve; numerous problems may come to the forefront. Sometimes one parent might be disengaged, and conflict during bedtime gets the nonparticipating parent off the couch. In these situations, it's important to resolve what is contributing to that parent's reluctance to be involved (principle 4: be patient).

Older Children

As your child grows older, she will probably want more input regarding her bedtime. This will require additional problem solving. You want her to get enough sleep, but without feeling forced into something unpleasant. Often the issue comes down to getting sufficient rest to meet obligations and maintain health and getting enough time awake to finish what she wants to do. You might say, "How much sleep do you want in order to feel good in the morning?" or "Is it worth it to you to give up your sleep to read that chapter?" (principle 8: establish "buy in").

Rather than letting your child stay up late to watch a TV program, it may work out better if you record the program for her to watch another day. You might also encourage her to complete schoolwork earlier so that she will have more time to enjoy herself when other family members are available later in the evening. Try to establish a nighttime routine that permits personal time and positive time with the rest of the family. However, make sure you have some availability for such time, or negative attention provoking could increase.

Tip

Forcing your child to try to sleep is unlikely to yield positive results or help her relax. If she complains that she is not ready to sleep, rather than tell her to turn off the light and lie in bed anyway, encourage her to do a quiet activity in her room until she becomes tired. Tell her that if she is having trouble sleeping, she can always get out of bed and (for example) read in a chair (it's helpful if the bed is associated only with sleeping). If she stays up too late and is irritable the next day, that outcome might help her shut down earlier.

Difficulty Caring for Personal Belongings

If your child likes for you to pick up after her, she may not show due respect and care for personal belongings. Without regard to the mess that she creates, she may throw playthings to the side as soon as they disappoint her, leaving a trail of her belongings all over the house. You do not want to forever behave like her personal servant, so it's important that your child take responsibility for her possessions.

Solutions

If you observe people who keep things neat and clean, you will probably notice that they consistently do three behaviors. First, they do some cleaning up before a mess becomes unwieldy. Second, when they are finished with an activity, they clean up so that the space is usable for something else. Third, they return items to their designated places when they are no longer using them. This keeps the items safe and easily found. Staying organized is not rocket science. It merely requires doing these routines.

When teaching your child to care for her possessions, help her get into the habit of picking up before the mess is overwhelming and prior to starting something new. You can ease back after she learns when it's permissible to leave things out. Let her know, "These toys get put away before you play that game." If she has left behind her toys in the kitchen, direct her, "Please come to the kitchen and take your toys."

Promoting Self-Management

If your child is going to care for her personal belongings, she must give up the luxury of having someone else put things away for her. She must give up the benefit of having others scurry around trying to find what she cannot locate. And she must figure out what to do when she stops an activity that is not yet completed. Sometimes it's not worthwhile to put things away when there is a good reason to keep them handy—we all feel this way at one time or another.

Those who like things exceptionally neat and clean lean toward putting things away even if they might use them again soon. They do not mind the extra work, because they do not like the mess, and they are super-protective of their belongings. Your child, however, may prefer the opposite. She might avoid the extra work, live with the mess, and take the chance that items will get lost or damaged. Both extremes have their merits, and as is true in almost any aspect of life, a middle ground usually has the fewest drawbacks.

A person's organizing behavior may also vary depending on the importance of protecting a specific item, the difficulty of the cleanup, and the consequences of living with the mess. For example, a disheveled bedroom or playroom has different repercussions than the same untidiness in the middle of the kitchen floor. All of this may sound complicated, but it means that your child must learn different behaviors in different circumstances.

Set firm limits. I guarantee that your child will be careless with her belongings if she has too many. She will less likely protect her belongings if you replace them too easily. She will not care where she puts them if you retrieve what she forgets. And she will have no trouble with the mess she creates if you pick up for her.

While some children are too harried or troubled to exert the energy and spend the time to be conscientious with personal belongings, many expect their parents to pick things up for them. They also assume that their parents will find or replace lost articles. Often weakness in discipline allows the carelessness to continue (see "Accommodation," in chapter 3).

So if you feel that your child is treating you like a maid or butler, stand tall and remain steadfast. If she does not pick up her candy wrappers, for example, say, "I love you a lot, and I am upset only a little, but I keep finding candy wrappers all over the house." Ask for her input to solve the problem, but if nothing improves, say, "I don't know what else to do, except stop buying candy until I see that you are picking up after yourself."

If your child continues to leave toys on the floor, talk with her about the burden of managing so many belongings at once. You can say: "Let's put these toys in storage so you'll have fewer to take care of. We can add more toys when all that stuff won't be such a hassle for you to deal with." You can also let her know that leaving toys underfoot gives you the message that the toys are not very important to her. Point out, "Unless you have a better idea, I may put the toys in storage to get them out of everyone's way." If you end up taking that action, and she complains, you may say something like "They're in the attic. I didn't think you cared about them because they were just lying there for days" (principle 9: assert yourself).

Too much emphasis on cleaning up after oneself, however, can lead to your child's refusing to clean a mess unless she made it. Your child may learn to say, "I'm not putting it away—I didn't leave it out," because she hears you saying the very same thing. In this case you could respond that sometimes helping others is not enabling them to be lazy. Sometimes a mess is not due to negligence, and there is no downside if everyone pitches in and lends a hand.

Tip

Set aside for your child a special place for belongings that are inconvenient to keep in her room. This will give her easy access to important items without infringing on others' rights to a clean space. She may also appreciate the fact that you are considering her point of view when you clear out space that is "just for her."

Exercise: Teach Your Child to Organize (Ages 5–10)

Ask your child to gather her favorite action figures, dolls, or hobby items (e.g., interlocking blocks, art supplies). Have her organize the items into different groups, and find out her reasons for grouping the items in a particular way. Then, if she is willing, have her assist you in organizing and storing some of *your* belongings. Finally, if she is willing, have her use her new skills to arrange some of *her* belongings, and marvel at her expertise.

Exercise: Provide Practice Making Cleaning Decisions (Ages 5–8)

Think of a situation in which a cleaning decision is necessary. Ask your child what she would do to solve the problem. Talk with her about the pros and cons of her decision. Then think of other situations for her to consider. Draw from actual experiences or make up a problem that has not yet occurred. Vary how easy it is to clean up versus the risk and inconvenience of leaving a mess. Here are some examples.

- *"You're playing with your paints on the floor, and you have to stop for dinner. You have a pet dog, and you know that you'll be finishing your painting as soon as dinner is over. What do you do?"*

- *"You just got a new model that you want to put together on the playroom table. You won't be able to finish it until tomorrow. Do you leave it in pieces on the table?"*

- *"You and your friend made a fort with pillows and blankets in the living room. Now your friend has to go home, but he wants to come back tomorrow to finish playing. What do you do?"*

Poor Money Management

Children and adults diagnosed with ADHD have a reputation for spending money irresponsibly. The situation may get so bad that their parents and spouses end up managing their money for them. While some people think that people with ADHD cannot recognize the longer-term consequences of frivolous spending, there is another way to understand the problem: As with other limits they neglect, people with ADHD do not abide by money-managing limits. They are less likely to say no to what they want. Your job, of course, is to change this behavior in your child.

Your child, however, may feel powerless in relation to money. She probably depends on you to give her access to money, and even when she has her own money, you may find it wise to oversee her purchases. You want her to develop financial responsibility and learn to save on her own, but you also want her to experience the pleasure of spending. Finding a comfortable balance is not always easy.

Without question, your child's experiences will influence her handling of money. If you spend money irresponsibly, she may copy those behaviors. If she has a never-ending supply of money, she will never say no to a purchase. She will have no reason to save, because money seems to "grow on trees." If you bail her out too frequently when she does not have money, she will also not learn to set money aside. She will assume that you will recompense her. And if she enjoys being dependent on you, she may keep herself poor and needy (see "Accommodation," in chapter 3).

To encourage sound money management, help your child recognize that everyone in the family must live within a budget: there is only a certain amount of money available for purchases. Even very young children can grasp this. As soon as your child understands the concept of "not enough," she can begin to understand the principle of insufficient funds.

Personal Money

It's now common practice to give a child personal money at age four or five. You can hold your child's personal money for her and keep a record on a piece of paper that she can easily see. It's important that you be consistent and give her the money you have allocated without making her ask you for it. It's also helpful if you keep accurate records. This shows her that you are reliable, and it begins teaching her how to keep a bankbook. If she knows how much money she has saved, she will also know how much she can spend. When you think she is ready, turn the money over to her so that she learns to keep it safe and organized on her own.

Instead of giving your child an allowance for the completion of a specific chore or specific chores (especially for work that is not out of the ordinary), give her an allowance simply because she is part of the family. This approach avoids the possible side effect that she will not help unless you offer payment. It also helps her learn about budgeting and spending wisely, because you will ask her to use her personal money to make certain purchases (e.g., a new doll for her collection). You then decide what kind of contribution you want her to make with her own funds (e.g., pay half of the cost of the doll).

Emphasize that family members usually help each other without payment. Although your child's allowance does not depend on it, the family assumes that she will behave in a considerate fashion because that is the "family way." If she is not behaving in that manner, try to find out why, but don't keep subsidizing her if she is behaving selfishly and taking advantage of others (principle 9: assert yourself).

When you feel that your child is freeloading, it may be reasonable to reduce her allowance. You can casually explain your actions by saying, "If you'd rather not pitch in, we can use your share of money to pay someone else to help us out." Let her know that failure to lend a hand imposes on others. Make it clear; you would like it if she wanted to join in, but it's also important that you make sure that there is no exploitation in the household.

A similar problem occurs when your child keeps taking things from others, loses her belongings, or is destructive. Let her know that you must hold her accountable, because this protects the rights of others. Say, "We need your money to help pay for the loss." This helps her learn to be more conscientious and to explore less costly ways to resolve her irritability. Likewise, if she has a tendency to be reckless in a store, caution her, "Have your bankbook ready because they'll charge you for anything that breaks."

<hr>

Tip

Encourage your child to save by making it difficult for her to borrow. This will more effectively help her learn about limits and preparation for the future. But proceed gently when you think she is making a questionable purchase. If you know that she intended to accumulate enough money to buy a video game but is preparing to buy something else, you might say, "I guess you decided not to save for the video game." When you intervene in this way, you give her the message that you see her as competent and that *she knows* she is making a significant dent in her savings. You are merely suggesting that she reconsider.

<hr>

Eating Problems

Your worrying about your child's eating can create a drama that she may not want to give up. Parents of children born prematurely find themselves in this predicament all the time. Their doctors instruct them to make sure their infant gains weight, and they get into the habit of pushing the child to eat from day one.

Eating can easily become a war of wills. You want your child to eat in healthy ways, but that requires her to make good food decisions. Blocking access to food, using food as a reward or punishment, criticizing her eating behaviors, using food to keep her busy, or forcing her to eat certain foods may seem to resolve the problem on the surface. However, those parenting behaviors can increase overeating, sneaking food, refusal to eat, and power struggles. You may end up contributing to atypical eating behaviors rather than minimizing them.

Solutions

Make it a family ritual to eat together at a table, and make mealtime a pleasure so that your child wants to be there. You do not want to turn eating into an uncomfortable experience. So don't pressure her to eat extra helpings or require her to eat all the food on her plate. You may create problems if you express feeling slighted or annoyed when she is not interested in the food you serve. So if she is not hungry for what you have prepared, just wrap up the food and let her know that she can eat it later, if she wants.

Rather than criticizing the amount she eats, ask, "What is a healthy amount for one portion?" This approach includes her in decision-making and treats her respectfully. If you think she is taking too much and depriving others, ask her to help you serve the food and figure out a way to allocate portions.

Help her understand the benefits of eating small amounts of certain foods; see whether you can agree on how much to eat in one sitting. Instead of berating her with the comment, "That many sweets will make you fat," you could say, "If you're hungry, maybe we have something better for you to eat." As always, the key is to develop an arrangement that works for both of you, because you cannot always monitor what she puts in her mouth. As the saying goes, "You can lead a horse to water, but you can't make her drink."

Not bringing certain foods into the house can also be a way to promote healthy eating. Out of sight, out of mind. However, you also want your child to make good food choices even when unhealthy food is there for the taking. So instead of taking her Halloween candy from her, which implies that she has no self-control, help her figure out an acceptable way to manage the sweets.

When promoting healthy eating, rather than say, "You can't eat dessert unless you eat your vegetables," say, "It's better for us to eat these foods first." Let her know, "Dessert is something we eat if we have a little room left at the end." Point out, "We all eat the healthier foods first to make sure our bodies get what they need." Everyone operates with the same limits; you are not trying to deny or control her when you talk about ways to eat.

You can also increase her say-so with food by requesting her input during grocery shopping. Preparing foods in ways that she enjoys will also reassure her that you acknowledge her preferences. However, overaccommodating to finicky eating can unfortunately create atypical eating behaviors that are detrimental over time.

Finicky Eating

Making a special meal for your child can be a way to show her you love her, but when you constantly cater to her whims, she may not learn to adjust to what the *family* is doing. And this will not help her when she ventures into the outside world. For example, other people may not be willing to "jump through hoops" for your child. Then it may be uncomfortable for her to eat at a friend's or cousin's house. You may also keep her from trying new foods when you continuously adjust into her narrow range of choices. These concerns are important.

One option is to allow your child to make her own meal when you disagree over food choices. However, if she chooses that path, it's important that she clean up afterward. You could say: "I already cooked a full meal for the family. If you want something different, you can make yourself a sandwich as long as you clean up right away." Your response gets her to question whether her complaining is worthwhile.

Risk

An ADHD diagnosis usually means that your child is very active. However, with those high activity levels, there is risk as well as fun. Your child may enjoy the excitement, freedom from limits, and heightened attention that occurs when her "motor is revving," but the side effect can be danger. That is what concerns you, especially when she responds to your attempts to protect her as stifling. Because there can be severe consequences when you do not stand in her way, it's easy to see how power struggles can escalate whenever children are active.

You want your child to enjoy the world and not live "in a bubble," but you also do not want her to injure herself. You want her to acknowledge that certain risks are not worth taking. However, if she thinks that you are too sheltering, she may stop listening to you altogether. If she thinks you caution her because you do not believe she can succeed, she may react defensively and dig in her heels. So tread carefully.

But even if your child has difficulty understanding the full impact of her actions, she does not have difficulty understanding that you are saying no. So what is stopping her from listening to you? Unless you can resolve that problem, you will have to be extremely vigilant if you want to shield her from harm. Yes, you can try to prohibit and physically restrain her, but unfortunately, that may not always be possible.

Curbing Risk

Few children want their parents to stop being concerned, so convey the message that you are advocating for her when you promote caution. Be clear that your concerns about safety often have to do with the lack of predictability in the world, not her level of competence. Let her know that you like to "play it safe" until you find out more about a situation. Ask her, "Would you help me figure out a careful way to do this?" (principle 3: take steps to address and resolve problems).

Resolving Resistance

Despite your best efforts, resistance to safety requests can be difficult to break down, especially when siblings or peers have different limits. For example, your child may not want to wear a bicycle helmet when she sees that her friends do not wear helmets. She may worry about teasing. This may keep her from protecting herself and increase her reluctance to accommodate to your sound advice. When that happens, ask her, "What concerns you about the teasing?" and try to help her figure out a way to respond if others start to ridicule.

The goal is for your child to be comfortable with the recommended safety measure and understand its advantages. Her following through is doubtful unless that is accomplished. In an attempt to increase "buy in," you could ask her, "Why do you think people _____ [wear a helmet, wear safety goggles, etc.] when they do this activity?" (principle 5: suspend judgment). When she states the benefits herself, she may be more willing to take the precautions.

Helping Your Child Distinguish Control vs. Protection When Reducing Risk (Ages 5–10)

Your child may be more receptive to safety limits if she sees the benefit rather than the denial. Here are some examples of how to turn an arbitrary limit into a message that you are acting to protect her when you advise a safety measure.

Limiting arbitrarily	Protecting
"You can't ride your bike without a helmet."	"Helmets aren't a choice—we all wear them. Let's find one you like so we can take care of that great brain of yours." "We like you too much to take any chances." "This isn't a risk that the family is willing to take."
"You have to hold my hand when we cross the street."	"Would you let me know when it's safe to cross?" "If we hold hands we can protect each other."
"You have to stay out of the living room so you don't break things and hurt yourself."	"Some things in the living room break easily. Let's find a better place for you to let loose."
"You're too young to watch that movie."	"They made that movie for older people. It's not that fun for kids."
"You have to wear protective gear when you skateboard."	"Others don't always see you, and the sidewalks are in bad shape." "Professionals always use protective gear."
"You can play with that toy only when I'm with you."	"If I'm with you, I can help if anything comes up that we're not prepared for."

The Next Step

Now you have learned ways to promote your child's self-care without constant reminders and coercion. When your child knows she can complete tasks without your help, she will be more secure and confident. The next step is to help your child interact with the family in a kind and caring fashion. Because her experiences within the family will likely be a powerful influence on her behavior outside the family in both the immediate and the long term, you want her experiences to serve her well.

6 Reducing ADHD Behavior in the Family

You have probably noticed that your child shows fewer ADHD behaviors when he is doing exactly what he wants. It's when he must accommodate to others' wishes that problems occur. Because family life requires accommodating, ADHD behaviors show up frequently in family groups. This chapter will help you learn to reduce your child's ADHD behavior within the household. A good first step is to develop a trusting relationship.

Trust

Without knowing it, you may have given your child a message of distrust very early. Like many parents, you probably childproofed your house to keep him safe and to prevent household items from being broken. However, when you continually resolve safety problems in this fashion, you are treating your child as unable to control himself. Your approach may not develop his self-restraint, and there is an undercurrent of not trusting him to do what is right, proper, and safe.

In addition, your child's active nature may frequently draw negative attention from you. You may spend much of your time chasing after and restricting him, and he may have learned to try to outmaneuver you using evasion and deception. The conflict, frustration, and lack of trust in your relationship can result in both of you feeling bad about yourselves and each other.

How to Develop Trust

If you can build a trusting relationship with your child in which you resolve the problems of day-to-day family life in a mutually agreeable way, your child will have less to gain from avoidance or the overstepping of bounds. Your goal is to treat him as competent to self-manage within the limits that work for both of you and trust that he will do what is right. A positive demeanor will help him cooperate more often, follow your directions more consistently, and coordinate with you more precisely.

You can begin developing trust by teaching your child to "look but don't touch." If he picks up an object he is not supposed to, instead of taking it from him (unless it poses a clear danger), ask him to put it back where it was and thank him for leaving it be (remember principle 1: use coercion as a last resort). Grabbing it from him will only make him want it more and give him the message that you do not trust him to put it back on his own. If he does not comply, calmly take the object away. You can then try handing it back (as soon as he settles down, if necessary) and asking him to put it where he found it. Whenever possible, it's better to have faith in his competency to follow the instruction and comply than to deny him the chance. Of course, if he continues to test your limits, you must be firm and keep the object from him. You may even have to use force to hold him back from grabbing it again. However, if you give him a chance to be trustworthy, and he succeeds, your accomplishment is greater.

As your trust increases, you can allow your child access to more objects and activities without being fearful that you are taking extraordinary risks. In this way, you gradually teach him to tolerate limits with less blocking and monitoring. You increase his freedom to operate without supervision and lay the foundation for self-management in a broader array of situations.

Reducing Sneaking, Stealing, and Lying

The most popular way to keep a child from fraudulent behavior is to threaten punishment. That intervention works fine as long as you are likely to catch him and he fears the consequence. However, as you know, you are not always privy to his actions, and there are many opportunities for him to operate "under the radar."

Sadly, many parents disregard this problem and try to stop dishonesty by constructing a system of punishments. They think that if the consequences are extreme enough, the risk of wrongdoing is not worth taking. Perhaps they are right, but that way of disciplining can have unwanted side effects. Their child may continue to be afraid of their reactions, and that uneasiness can make it difficult for the child to be forthright with them (see "Avoidance," in chapter 3).

When there is wrongdoing, you most certainly want your child to make amends and rectify damages. You may also want to block him from certain activities until you are comfortable that he will not repeat the misconduct. However, it's important to resolve the reasons for his transgression and help him find other ways to respond to the same situation in the future.

But your child may not be open with you if you are threatening and punitive. Those responses from you can trigger fabrications and other forms of avoidance, creating a divide between you and your child. Your child may not want to speak about what happened. For example, if you ask him, "Did you take my tools?" in an accusing way, you may get an immediate denial. However, if you ask, "Would you help me find my tools and put them away?" or "Would you help me figure out a way to keep these tools safe and organized?" you may get a more favorable response.

Ways to Address Sneaking, Stealing, and Lying (Ages 6–12)

Asking the following kinds of questions may help reduce deception a lot better than focusing solely on increasing your child's fear of punishment. As you may know, some people never show integrity no matter how much punishment they receive. Your job is to make it safe for your child to disclose questionable behavior and to address the source of the problem together.

- "How do you feel about stealing from us?"

- "What made it so important for you to do that?"

- "What would be another way to handle that situation?"

- "Will telling me exactly what happened help us solve the problem? Would you like to give it a try?"

- "What would be so terrible if I said no and you didn't do it?"

- "Was something bothering you when you did that?"

- "Are you feeling left out or cheated in some way?"

- "Instead of sneaking, what if you came to me and we tried to work it out together?"

- "What kind of relationship would you like us to have with each other?"

  - "How can we get that to happen?"

  - "What's getting you to be afraid of me?"

  - "What do you think I'd do if you told me what went on?"

- "Even if no one will catch you doing something wrong, is there a benefit to being honest?"

- "Would you like to leave your stuff out and have it be safe? Would you like to do the same for others?"

Triangles in the Family

ADHD behavior can occur during one-to-one interactions when your child faces adversity, but you can more easily make adjustments to contain ADHD behavior when it's just you and your child. When more people are involved, things can become more difficult, and ADHD behavior is likely to increase. That is why it's important to manage your child effectively when a third person is involved.

When a group breaks into two against one, we say that a "triangulation" is occurring. Triangles can put strain on relationships and interfere with cooperation. Because a child with ADHD often shows excessive behavior, conflict can be extreme when he is part of a triangle. Resentment from other family members and not knowing whether to hold your child accountable for his misdeeds can worsen the problem. Sometimes you may coddle and protect him because you feel that he is weak and disabled with ADHD. At other times, you may blame him for creating problems that wear on you. The inconsistency of your response can reduce the effectiveness of your parenting. So let's examine some triangles that commonly occur in families and identify effective ways to cope with them.

Sibling Conflict

If your child has a sibling, the two may argue and compete with each other. Typically, children learn very quickly that conflict between them pulls you in. Yes, they are arguing about something, but usually, they know how to avoid an escalation when they want to. Creating controversy that will include you is often their primary motivation to fight, and it usually follows a predictable script: One will approach the other and begin to antagonize in the customary way. The other will notice the signal and retaliate as usual. The basic theme of the conflict is "who gets whom into trouble?" They do very little to resolve the problem on their own, and it spirals in intensity until you get involved. Their fighting has the powerful effect of getting you to stop what you are doing, and it can sabotage your agenda. They know that you want them to get along, and the fighting "takes the wind out of your sails." What a potent tool they have at their disposal. They get to release their irritability and hold you hostage in the process.

In your attempts to stop the discord, at times you may support one child or the other. While you may be trying to promote fairness, this approach is unlikely to be effective in reducing conflict. Taking sides rarely helps. This is because the child you advocate for will like the help that you give him, while the other child will dislike the fact that you sided against him. He will feel devalued and become angry. Your disapproval toward him will magnify his resentment toward his sibling, who will then be seen as the cause of his suffering. More than ever, he will want to mistreat his sibling and punish both of you. He knows that mistreating his sibling is bothersome, and he will use it as a weapon. Even when he anticipates punishment, he will continue to be unkind because he will not want to let his sibling (or you) get the best of him. He may accuse you of favoritism, and you may want to defend yourself. However, when you try to convince him that his allegations are false, you may unknowingly reinforce him to keep attacking your integrity. This is because he likes it when you start to focus on his sibling's shortcomings and reassure him that you do care about him.

Interestingly enough, the protected sibling is often the first to physically strike. He continues to instigate because he knows he can count on your support. He is typically getting back at his sibling for mistreating or neglecting him, and he obtains a sense of importance when you rush to his aid. Unfortunately, he gains it at the expense of his sibling, and this damages his relationship with his sibling even more.

Perhaps you think you can identify the victim and the perpetrator when you rush in to arbitrate. However, often sibling conflicts have been going on for years. So how do you know who started the problem? Sometimes you may jump to the wrong conclusion, and this will further alienate the child you accuse. So remember principle 5: suspend judgment.

It's also important to be aware that a personal bias may influence your decision to protect one of the children. For example, if one of the children is behaving similarly to your spouse (or your parent or sibling) in a way that you dislike, you may be less sympathetic toward that child. Your history influences your reactions, and your relationship with that child worsens when you respond in a biased fashion.

Sibling Alliance

Sometimes the child with ADHD and his sibling will antagonize you together. When they feel the same way about a problem, they may unite forces and gang up against you. For example, if they dislike your impatience in the morning, they will both move slowly and not complete necessary tasks, as a way to push back. They can bring you to the point where you dislike your own behavior, and you question whether you were too severe. You may end up apologizing and feeling guilty that you have sent them to school upset and worry about it all day. Boy, are they good at what they do.

Stepfamily and Birth Family

If your child has a stepparent or stepsiblings, triangles can be quite intense. When your child with ADHD and your new partner or new children have conflict, you are in the unenviable position of having to choose between supporting your new family members or protecting your child. The tendency is for birth family members to support each other and assign blame to the newcomers. Your partner may accuse you of favoritism and being too lenient, and you may feel that your partner is too harsh and uncaring. Often blood runs thicker than water, and your relationship with your partner suffers when you side with your child.

Child-Parent Alliance

Another triangle occurs when you have conflict with your child and your partner rushes to your child's defense. Your partner may identify with your child because he is upset with you for the same reason as your child. For example, if he thinks you are too rigid and controlling, he may automatically side with your child when he hears an argument about limits. To counteract your parenting style, he goes to the opposite extreme.

The sad part is that your child learns to cooperate with you even less when this triangle occurs. He sees someone else complaining about your actions, and he imitates the negativity. Your partner's behavior has the regrettable consequence of teaching your child to be resistive toward you and perhaps other authority figures as well.

Child in the Middle

An important and very serious triangle occurs when parents identify the child with ADHD as the source of family unhappiness. Because he has difficult behavior, it's very easy for him to get into that box. Often one or both parents feel that it's necessary to aid and rescue their partner when the child misbehaves.

On occasion, however, the child's parents might be angry at each other but not resolving their relational problems in a direct fashion. It becomes easier for them to complain about their child rather than confront each other about what is wrong. Yes, he may be difficult to manage and creating a lot of stress for the family. He may even prefer bringing his parents together and having them harp on him instead of arguing with each other. But he is unfortunately in the middle of an unresolved problem between two distressed adults.

Resolving Sibling Conflict

You can see how triangles harm relationships and ignite many ADHD behaviors. They may reinforce your child for being annoying, dependent, or avoidant. That is why it's important to get the triangles to stop.

Be neutral. Taking sides will only make matters worse. Yes, this might not be fair, especially if you think one person is clearly in the wrong, but you have a better chance of being effective in the end when you hold a middle ground. Try to defuse the conflict by creating some separation between the warring parties, but don't criticize or assign blame. When stopping an ongoing conflict between children, for example, don't call out one child's name or speak only to one of them. That child may think that you are blaming him. Speak calmly to both children simultaneously.

Increase calmness. If the children are upset, you might delay problem solving until they are calmer and better able to think clearly. Your initial step is to prevent further aggression and soothe injuries. But do as little as possible, because you want the children to do the bulk of the work to resolve the conflict. For example, you could say, "Everybody keep hands and feet to themselves," "In our family we don't hit each other," or "I'm going to stop both of you right now."

Model diplomacy. The next step is to see whether the children are interested in resolving the problem they are having. If not, then find out what is stopping them from making up. It's difficult to move forward if the children are not willing to make amends. Otherwise, you get into a difficult situation in which you are working alone to decrease hard feelings. When they are agreeable to peacemaking, you can model diplomacy by asking, "What might work for both of you?" or "How do you wish it could be with each other?"

It's important that the warring parties identify what they are fighting about, and you want them to find a way to reconcile. If they look at you, complain, and make accusations, redirect them to talk calmly with each other about the changes that they would like to see happen. If one child has limited verbal skill, you may have to speak for that child, but always remain impartial and ask the children how they feel about each other's ideas.

Stay on track. If the children keep identifying alternatives that are problematic (e.g., "Let's give my little brother away"), avoid the attempt to keep the fight going. Stay calm and don't feed into the drama. Let their complaints roll off you like water on a duck's back. Sometimes a child will disagree with very reasonable ideas presented by his sibling because he does not want his sibling to get credit for having solved the problem. Positive behavior from one child will often result in the other child becoming more negative. People often get irritated when they feel that they are losing ground.

Tip

When the children are stuck, help them identify the theme of the argument. You might say, "This may be one of those times when one of you wants to play and the other is disappointed," or "Maybe you're taking your anger out on each other because we're not going to the park." Just get them started, and then work together to uncover the different reasons for their emotionally charged responses (including whether they are angry with you or someone else).

Be proactive. Often you can reduce conflicts by attending to the children before the fighting starts. If you must do an activity that takes your attention away from them, notify them that you will be busy. For example, "I was thinking of giving my friend Julia a call." The children might appreciate that you considered them and thus adapt better when you are talking with your friend.

The key is to resolve problems before there is conflict. This includes encouraging family members to voice opinions more often instead of waiting until their anger intensifies. Let them know that there does not have to be a crisis in order for them to express their desires and feelings.

You can also let the children know that a peaceful family is better for everyone. Not only does peace increase the family's happiness and safety, it's easier to have guests in the house when everyone is getting along. When family relationships are positive (and his self-esteem is high), your child with ADHD is also more likely to be respectful in front of others.

Be patient. Ending long-standing family conflict is never easy. If you stop taking sides, problems may worsen at first. The children may initially think that they must fight more to get the results that are familiar to them. The formerly protected child may wonder whether you have forgotten him, and his sibling may become more aggressive. He may think that he now has the freedom to bully. Both children will keep testing to see whether you revert to your old pattern. The fighting may escalate, and you may think you are on the wrong track. You might even find that the other child starts behaving poorly as soon as your child with ADHD settles down. However, staying neutral and promoting compromise will help over time, so stay the course. Triangles do not cause ADHD, but they surely interfere with efforts to reduce ADHD behavior.

Exercise: You Are the Ambassador (Ages 5–12)

When resolving family quarrels, aim to be a mediator, not an enforcer. The next time there is a family dispute, pretend you are an ambassador. Your government does not care how the clash is resolved, but they want it to end. Your reputation for good work depends on it. Here are some skills that effective ambassadors use:

- *Neutrality is essential; you win only if both parties are happy.*

- *View the problem as if you were sitting in the balcony of a theater.*

- *After one party speaks, encourage the other to repeat back what was said. This helps the parties develop empathy. (Listening shows caring.) When necessary, model this for them.*

- *Watch for discomfort and encourage the parties to voice what is bothering them.*

- *Perspectives are neither right nor wrong; help the parties find ways to accommodate to each other's preferences.*

- *Help each party understand the history of the other. This will help them understand why certain preferences are important and why certain sensitivities occur.*

- *Clarify the problem and encourage all parties to offer solutions.*

- *Explore any idea that will help produce an acceptable compromise.*

Contributing and Working Together

How do you get your child to contribute to the family instead of showing ADHD behavior? If you want your child to do more for others as he grows older, it's important to encourage him to help the family as early as possible. If you do too much for him for too many years, it will be difficult for him to make this transition. It's not always easy for a child to discover the joy of assisting others, but it's usually beneficial to model the behaviors you want him to copy. Let him know, "In our family we help each other." When you notice a lack of contribution, remind him that relationships are a two-way street. You might say, "We're willing to lend you a hand—why not do the same for us?"

Exercise: Resolve Exploitation and Share Responsibility (Ages 5–10)

Keeping a household running smoothly takes a lot of work, and sometimes you may not get the cooperation that you want when doing certain tasks. Think about a situation that comes up often and leaves you feeling exploited. Identify every detail that bothers you. For example, if you feel exploited over issues having to do with laundry, you might identify the following details about the situation that bother you:

- *You run around gathering dirty clothes.*

- *Your child uses too many towels or clothes each day.*

- *Your child expects to have something washed at his whim.*

- *Your child does not put away folded clothes and allows them to mix with dirty clothes.*

Then talk with your child about these problems. Ask whether he would like to take better care of you and work out a solution. If the answer is yes, then have a discussion about how the two of you can share the responsibilities of the task, or brainstorm changes you both can make that will make your lives easier. In the case of the laundry, you might come up with the following ways to resolve the problem:

- *You will do the laundry only on particular days.*

- *If your child wants something, he tells you by a certain deadline.*

- *You will wash only what is in the hamper.*

- *You will extend the courtesy of folding the clothes and bringing them to your child's bedroom as long as he continues to put them neatly away.*

- *You will decide what to do with items left in pockets.*

Helping Can Be a Pleasure

Being considerate of others does not have to be unpleasant. In fact, some people claim that someone who is kind will have a happier life. Helping can be an opportunity to assume leadership and a way to increase one's value to others. The helper is taking charge of something, and others are depending on him. He is a hero, not a slave. You can encourage this mind-set by saying things like the following:

- "We'd be very grateful if you helped us with this."

- "We couldn't have done it without you."

- "Your help saved me a lot of work."

On the other hand, if you tell your child that he *has* to do a chore, he may feel that you are requiring him to be submissive. He is likely to recoil, and you may spend your time struggling for power. If he feels that you are relegating him to an inferior status, he will be less eager to donate his time.

As a way to increase the value of helping, ask your child, "What would you like to take charge of?" or "What kind of contribution would you like to make?" Let him know that you are counting on him to handle certain tasks because he has the know-how (principle 7: treat your child as competent to succeed). Informing him ahead of time about doing exceptional tasks (e.g., shampooing the rugs) will make it easier for him to change his plans and lend a hand. You can also increase his commitment to help by asking him, "When would you like to start?" For daily or weekly tasks with other family members, ask the participants, "How will you both know whose turn it is?" or "How do you want to divvy up the jobs?"

Let your child know that his efforts free others to take charge of different activities so that no one gets overburdened. Each person pitches in so that the family operates like a well-oiled machine. Help him recognize that his contribution gives the family extra time and money to do a variety of other desirable activities. For example, compliment him by saying "Because you picked up the yard during the week, we can leave for the beach earlier on Saturday."

Stay Positive

If you pester or complain, your child will dislike the hassling and criticism. This may increase his avoidance and unwillingness to help. He may stop trying and let you handle it on your own, complaining "I can't do it right" or "You're never happy with the job I do." While this might be his excuse to avoid the work, your interactions may be feeding the negativity.

A common example of this problem occurs when a child has asked to learn a musical instrument: his lessons start out positively, but if his parents start to badger him about practicing, his interest starts to wane. His parents obviously only want him to make progress, but the nagging clearly does not increase his effort. What might have happened if his parents had instead asked him to give the family a recital when he was ready? The invitation would have enhanced his status, and he would have gained notoriety for having acquired new skills. Helping the family is very similar. Your child will raise his social standing when he makes life easier for others. The focus on his contributions will spark his desire to give more.

You may also find that you get better results when you allow your child to complete a job the way he chooses. When he achieves without your orchestration, he gains confidence that he can do it on his own. If you wait for him to seek your help and ask a question, he will be more receptive to suggestions about how to improve.

Increase Independence and Initiative

When your child is not doing his part, and you think he could use some coaxing, give him a prompt, but keep it vague. Telling him exactly what to do prevents him from using his own resources. For example, if you know the dog needs to be fed, you could say: "I was thinking about Fido. I wonder whether he's getting hungry."

Instead of telling your child "Pick up that piece of paper," "Shut the door," "Flush the toilet," or "Don't wake us up so early" each time the problem occurs, help him learn a general procedure so he can show the desired behavior without any cueing the next time. Your guidance can have a far-reaching effect if you say, "Whenever you see paper on the floor, it would be helpful if you picked it up," "Whenever you're the last one in the room, please close the door," or "We flush each time, to be considerate." This beats saying "Go back and flush" day in and day out. When he acknowledges the general idea and says, "Yes, I'll do it each time," you know he is getting the message. Later on, reinforce his following through by saying "I noticed that you picked up that paper and threw it away," "It's great that you're letting us sleep late on weekends," or "Thanks for shutting the door behind you." These interactions help your child manage his own behavior and guide him to the admirable behavior of helping others *without* having to be asked. Think of how great it feels when your child shows initiative and helps just because he sees that you are struggling (e.g., when you are bringing in the groceries). How would you like to experience more of that warm feeling?

Exercise: Develop a Family Culture of Helping (Ages 5–10)

Together with your child, identify the ways that family members have been considerate and helpful toward each other during the week. Here is an example.

Samantha (mother):	Your dad warmed up the car for me.
Amy (child):	You looked for art supplies for me when you were at the mall.
Samantha:	You left me a note that you fed the dog so I didn't feed him twice.
Amy:	Dad was always on time to pick me up at my games.

Working through Obstacles

Unfortunately, there are benefits to not helping. If you ask your two children to pick up their toys, for example, one child may comply while the other ignores your request. In many instances, the child who is not helping draws most of the attention. His refusal disrupts you and sabotages the other child's opportunity to be in the limelight. To avoid this problem, pay more attention to the child who is giving assistance. But don't exaggerate your appreciation, because this is likely to create additional bitterness.

If no one agrees to help, you have yet another problem on your hands. You may have to do the cleaning yourself. You might politely say, "Maybe next time you'll be willing to put things away," or "It will be easier for me to do this again if I know that you'll pick up when we finish." While you hope to get a positive response, you may be stuck "holding the bag." You could threaten, but your best bet is to avoid getting into lopsided arrangements (taking out too many games at once, permitting easy access to every dish and utensil, etc.) until your child demonstrates that he will share the cleaning workload. Similar to putting toys in storage, you can reduce the number of objects at his disposal until you are confident that he will contribute to the upkeep.

Exercise: Identify the Advantages of Family Routines (Ages 5–10)

Your child will be encouraged to behave in a certain way if he understands the benefits. First, identify a routine that you advocate. Then ask your child, "Why is it good to do that?" For example, what are the advantages to his making his bed, picking up after eating, struggling before asking for help, and getting dressed before playing in the morning? Encourage your child to think of as many reasons as he can.

For example, here are some reasons your child may think of to keep the playroom clean:

- *It's easier to find things.*

- *It's more comfortable for guests.*

- *There's more space to play.*

- *I don't have to go back later and clean.*

- *The mess won't get too big.*

- *I know what I have, so I don't buy it again.*

- *My parents don't mind the toys because they are put away.*

- *My brother will lend me toys because I keep them safe.*

Problems with Schedules and Transitions

You can think of time as the ultimate limit. Time governs our lives and helps us coordinate with each other. That is why it's important that your child respond to time limits in an acceptable way. However, your child probably responds to time the same way he responds to the many other limits that he encounters: he neglects. Often you design and maintain schedules, and he continues to ignore the parameters you impose.

Coordinating "in time" usually requires a lot of cooperation. But this can be difficult when your child does not attend to when plans are established or is disinterested in participating (see "Avoidance," in chapter 3). Often he may be preoccupied with his own agenda and disregard your requests to stay together, unless of course he likes what will happen. His failure to participate can be a powerful way to stay in control, because he gains authority when you have to prod, chase, or wait for him to come.

Clearly, ADHD behaviors disrupt the pacing of family life. Your child either races ahead to get to what he wants before you are ready (see "Acquisition," in chapter 3) or lags behind and causes a delay. He is unavailable when you want him, and he holds you back when you are in a rush. He has no trouble transitioning when he likes the next activity (e.g., leaving to get ice cream), but he transitions slowly when he must give up what he prefers. Getting him ready to go to the park is far easier than getting him ready for school.

Solutions

You may feel that your child needs frequent repetition or a command to listen and look you in the eye to synchronize. However, his failure to coordinate with you gives him extra time to do what he wants and prevents you from dominating him. While pressure tactics may eventually get him to conform, this is not a great solution because other people will not want to work that hard to keep him in step.

Notify Ahead of Time

It's usually best to resolve problems before they occur. So if you know that your child will have trouble transitioning, talk beforehand. He may respond more positively if you give him adequate notification and recognize the importance of what he is doing. For example, if he is watching TV, you might say, "When the advertisement comes on, will you help us with the water bottles?" If it's not possible to give him a heads-up, you might still acknowledge his point of view by saying "I'm sorry to spring this on you when you're busy, but we have to leave right now."

Promote Accommodation

When your child is not transitioning, you can start the process without saying a word and hope that he will follow. Unless he is extremely preoccupied, he knows what you want him to do, but he is gaining too much from his failure to stay with you. He may also like the fact that you usually work hard to coax him. It may help him feel important, and he may keep lollygagging as long as he profits in that way. However, when it's imperative that he move along quickly, you can physically escort him to the next activity without showing any emotion (principle 2: stay calm).

But remember, wherever you go, rather than tug and pull, it's better for your child to transition on his own accord. Teach him to attend to the same transition signals that you rely on. These include a clock or alarm, others transitioning, or a request by someone to start another activity. Break his habit of requiring you to make a special effort to keep him with the group, for example by going to extremes to get him out of bed in the morning or pleading with him to come to the dinner table. Show him that staying coordinated has advantages. Make your time together enjoyable, and remove any benefit that accompanies his failure to stay "in the mix." You want him to learn that people will not always adjust to him or provide compensation when he neglects. He might instead suffer undesirable consequences. For example, the family might start the movie or eat without him rather than endlessly wait or keep calling his name.

The Buddy System

The aim is to help your child coordinate "in time" with less discomfort. For example, when you want him to tell you his whereabouts, it's not that you want to control him. Awareness of location permits both of you to find each other more easily. You could ask him, "Do you think it would be helpful for you to know where I am?" and explore the advantages that occur when you stay in touch. Because you are willing to inform him about *your* location, the arrangement is similar to any other "buddy system": it's a way to protect and care for each other. The intent is not to restrict or spy on him. You can highlight this by saying, for example, "Your father will often call me to stay in touch in this very same way."

You can encourage your child to contact you by phone at regular intervals and notify you of changes in plans. However, he may be reluctant to do so if he thinks you will invariably say no and require him to come home. Establishing a pattern of flexibility (when possible) will help offset these concerns.

But even when you take those precautions, your child may still see you as overprotective. He may think that you either doubt his ability to operate in the world without you or think he is not trustworthy. When that happens, explain, "I'm very cautious until there is a routine. Calling me lets me know that everything is fine." For additional encouragement, say, "You're taking really good care of me when you stay in touch and let me know you're running late." Your appreciation of his kindness and consideration will encourage him (principle 6: say it positively).

Tip

Avoid using the word "curfew," because it implies control and restriction. Instead, talk about coordinating "in time" as a way to "work as a team." Punctuality, notifying each other of changes in schedules, and waiting patiently are all ways to respect each other's priorities. Everyone benefits.

Exercise: Help Your Child Design a Schedule (Ages 5–10)

Your child will be more likely to comply with a schedule if he helps design it. Younger children can draw a comic strip of themselves doing the sequence of actions. Older children can write down the steps or dictate the sequence to you. A good place to start is the morning routine on school days. Smooth sailing in the morning will eliminate a lot of stress.

1. Ask your child to plan a morning routine for both of you.

2. Ask him to identify the sequence of steps and time that each segment starts and stops.

3. Ask him how he will keep track of time for each step in the process.

4. Ask him what he will do if he is running late or, conversely, has time to spare.

Resolving the Morning Routine

Morning routines demand strict adherence to time limits, because there can be significant consequences for being late. There could be reprimands from school, and you could be docked pay at your job. That penalty will mean less money for the family and fewer options for fun activities. When talking about these consequences with your child, emphasize that everyone suffers. Then ask, "Are you willing to help us get to work and school on time?"

Find Common Ground

You and your child are interdependent in the morning. For that reason, it's best to work out a morning routine that is acceptable to both of you. Let him know: "It's hard for me when you miss the bus in the morning. Can we solve that problem once and for all?" If your child can find a way to play video games or do other activities and still get out of the house according to schedule, then so be it.

Often it's easier to keep to a schedule if breakfast can wait until after all other morning activities are completed. Doing as much prep work as possible the night before is also helpful; last-minute harassing rarely speeds things up. If you think your child could benefit from a nudge, nonchalantly ask, "Are you going to school this morning?" As always, your child is more likely to cooperate when you are calm and respectful (principle 7: treat your child as competent to succeed).

Resolving Resistance

If your child is not doing the morning routine, there may be a variety of reasons. Morning conflict can be a powerful way to sabotage and avoid. Sometimes going to school may feel like getting ready for the guillotine. Identifying and resolving what is blocking your child's compliance is essential. He might do his routine flawlessly once you address what is getting in his way. You know that he is capable of being punctual. After all, he gets up and moves along just fine when he is going to do something fun, right? You may want to investigate the following possibilities.

- He is avoiding school because he is not prepared.

- Something is wrong at school.

- He is having difficulty separating from you.

- He is upset with you.

- He likes it when you do more for him when you are rushing.

If all else fails, you can try these solutions:

- If he misses the bus, have him pay for some of the gas that you use while driving him.

- Leave on time even if he is not ready. He can finish dressing or eating on the way to school.

- Wait patiently and allow natural consequences to play out. Schools have developed ways to deal with tardiness. If necessary, let the school know that you are doing this procedure.

Problems with Sharing and Perspective Taking

Your child probably does not share or take turns like his peers. He seems to forget the rules that others obey. Rather than attend to his own lapses, he notices only what others are doing wrong. He is unlikely to share blame any more than he shares household work, and he fails to see things from others' point of view. However, if he continues to profit from his self-centeredness, he is unlikely to change.

Solutions

To remedy your child's tendency to be self-absorbed, try to both resolve your child's concerns about others depriving him and make it more difficult for him to exploit others. Let him know he will benefit when he compromises, because relationships last longer and are more pleasurable when there is both give and take. Teach him to follow the Golden Rule and acknowledge others' perspectives. Point out the advantages of sharing: "You can keep it for yourself, or you can share and make a friend."

There are many opportunities for you to nurture sharing and consideration. For example, after you recognize your part in a problem, ask your child to identify his part in the problem as well. Ask, "What could you do differently so that things work out better for us the next time?" If you focus on both sides of the story, you help him learn a respectful and compassionate interpersonal style.

Finally, stop allowing your child to take advantage of you. That will help him learn to share and accommodate to others as he grows older. For example, you might say: "I haven't been getting enough time to use the computer. Let's figure out a way to share it so that we both are happy" (principle 3: take steps to address and resolve problems).

Exercise: Help Your Child Take Another Person's Perspective (Ages 7–12)

In this exercise, your child practices taking your perspective. This will help him maintain positive social relationships in the future. Select a recent problem that occurred between you. Take turns asking each other the following questions. Go back and forth until an acceptable compromise is established.

- *"What do you think upset me?"*

- *"What did I want you to do?"*

- *"What made it difficult for you to do what I wanted?"*

- *"What would help both of us feel better?"*

Etiquette

Teaching your child about etiquette is important. Good etiquette helps lay the groundwork for positive school behavior, because success in that setting also requires a lot of accommodating.

At one time or another, we all do things to make others comfortable, even if it's inconvenient for us. We dress a certain way, stay quiet while others talk, ask others to pass food instead of reaching, and do extra cleaning so guests will feel welcome. We allow others to go first, hold our utensils in particular ways, leave a room the same way we found it, and make people feel special on their birthday. You want your child to learn to do the same.

Ways to Develop Etiquette

Pleasing others can be enjoyable, but not if etiquette is associated with faultfinding and coercion. So instead of demanding that your child say "thank you," ask him whether he would *like* to thank a person who has been kind. Let him know, "I really love it when you say 'thank you' to me," or offer a suggestion: "I bet Roberta and Hank would really like it if you thanked them." This makes it easier for him to save face if he has forgotten his manners.

Rather than correct your child in front of others, defer to his judgment and gently ask, "What would be a polite way to handle this?" He may feel more willing and confident to show etiquette if you do not harp on him. Over time, his good manners will increase because others will compliment him and treat him kindly when he behaves politely.

Preparation Helps

As usual, talking beforehand is a good idea. For example, you might say: "When your aunt comes to visit, it's very important that we all be extra quiet. She is very sad, and we don't want to disturb her." Similarly, you could say: "Your grandmother spent a lot of time finding a present for you. She might really like it if you thanked her a lot."

You can nurture etiquette when you notice your child's politeness and model good manners in front of him, including treating him courteously when he is entertaining friends. He may also learn more quickly if you involve him in etiquette decisions when making plans for guests. For example, you could ask him, "How can we make sure everyone gets a turn?" This kind of practice will help him develop into a first-rate host.

Exercise: The Pleasing the Guest Game (Ages 6–10)

This exercise teaches your child to be a competent host. Before someone comes to visit, talk with your child about doing these five obliging behaviors with a guest.

1. Waiting or hurrying for the guest

2. Permitting the guest to go first

3. Doing what the guest wants to do

4. Making sure the guest is comfortable

5. Making sure the guest feels included

After the visit ends, ask your child to recall when he did these things. List his successes and discuss how he felt. If you noticed a pleasing behavior that he did not mention, add that to the list. You reinforce him when you admire his accomplishments.

The Next Step

Now you have learned some basic ways to reduce ADHD behavior inside the home. Decreasing ADHD behavior outside the home is our next step. It's very important that your child learn mature self-management when he is in public. When he is in the outside world, you want his actions to be safe and respectful, and you want your travels together to be enjoyable. Let's see how we can get that to happen.

7 Managing ADHD Behavior Away from Home

You must eventually leave the house, so it's important to manage ADHD behavior in the outside environment. Traveling can be dangerous. Further, if your child oversteps bounds and causes damage to others' property, the result can be costly. You also risk not completing your errands and offending strangers when you do not curb your child's ADHD behavior. It would be great if she behaved herself, but how can you get that to happen?

Problems in the Car

The new relationship that you are forming with your child will help immensely wherever you go, but some unique problems may occur during car rides. Traveling while your child is misbehaving is both aggravating and dangerous. Sometimes you may be in a hurry, and if your child is unwilling to cooperate, she can sabotage everything.

Solutions

You want your child to put on her seat belt without being prompted, but if she is angry about something else, she may resist doing so. Looking into the source of her annoyance makes better sense than focusing only on her lack of compliance. Because the backseat can be lonely, you can also avoid negative attention–seeking by being proactive. You can include your child in a discussion, pack items of interest for her, or play a game with her so that the trip is less isolating and tedious.

If your child starts a commotion while you are driving, you may get anxious about safety. You may have to find a place to stop the car and wait for her to settle down. Yes, this might make you late, but it's your best option. Let your child know, "It's safe to drive only if we stay in our seats and get along." This approach is especially useful when you have more than one child riding with you. However, before you return to the road, make sure that the children have stopped fighting and are doing something different, even if it's only gazing out the window. The fighting may resume quickly if they are not distracted from the conflict.

Who Sits Where?

When there is frequent controversy about the seating arrangement in the car, apply the same procedures you would use to diminish fighting within the household (see chapter 6); help the children figure out the sharing system that they want to use. Do this ahead of your next trip: at a time when everyone is calm, ask the children whether they have any ideas to solve the problem. One child may have a special seating preference, but as long as the children figure out what works for them, all will be well. Make sure that their system accurately reminds them about who has first choice at particular times, or it's unlikely to be effective. You do not want to get stuck keeping track of whose turn it is for the preferred seat.

Using the Bathroom

Often trips are long, and it's not always easy to get to a restroom. Your child may insist that she does not need to go to the bathroom before you leave, but then, soon after leaving, she may start to complain that she needs to use the toilet. You can stop and quickly accommodate, but if the problem becomes repetitious, try to find a solution that eliminates the inconvenience. Let her know: "The trip is long, and it will be difficult to find a bathroom. Would you like to use the toilet now so that you'll be more comfortable while we drive?" If she says no, you could add, "We'd be happy to wait for you," as a way to gently get her to reconsider.

Help your child get into the habit of using the bathroom prior to leaving. Model what you want her to do, and ask her whether she wants to take a turn. Start the trip whether she goes or not. If events play out badly, there may be great inconvenience, but try to stay calm so that she pays attention to her own discomfort. Eventually, she will learn that she is better off copying your behavior, and you will not have to say a word about it.

Problems in the Store

Your child may be very cooperative when you are shopping for something that she wants. But her behavior may be dramatically different when she feels coerced to shop for others. As is often the case, your child's ADHD behavior is ignited and fueled when she loses the authority to determine what happens.

Solutions

Your child may cooperate better if you are in a good mood, so you have significant influence. Talking about your child's favorite subjects of discussion may also help make unwanted shopping less annoying. But most important, your child is likely to cooperate better if she has more input into what takes place (remember principle 8: establish "buy in"). For example, if you are grocery shopping, you can ask her whether she wants to assist you in deciding what to buy. Older children might enjoy helping you identify bargains. Others might like the job of reading the grocery list or driving the cart.

The bottom line is that ADHD behavior will be less frequent when you and your child are getting along positively and sharing authority. Try to find the "sweet spot" where you accommodate to her enough that she is comfortable accommodating to you so you can complete your errand. This is difficult to achieve, but it can be done, and it yields the greatest long-term impact on the frequency of ADHD behavior during shopping excursions.

Exercise: Let Your Child Design a Shopping Trip (Ages 6–10)

The next time you need to make a shopping trip with your child, ask her to help you plan. Perhaps she has some ideas about which store to go to first, what time to leave, or what items to buy. Perhaps she can help with money management so you stay within a budget.

Resolving Public Misbehavior

Things may not always go smoothly when you are out and about, so what do you do when your child acts up? You can ignore the behavior when possible or redirect her, but allowing her to be loud and disruptive is not always fair to others. There may also be risks that you do not want to play out when she is exuberant in public places.

Unfortunately, you may have to physically stop your child or leave the store when her behavior is intrusive or unsafe. In some instances, it may be possible to reenter the store after a short time, if your child settles herself and you feel assured that things will be positive when you return to the store.

However, sometimes you may have to go home. In these situations, it's important that your child recognize that her actions have a ripple effect. You can highlight these negative side effects. For example, "Because we didn't finish our shopping, we will have to go back later, and I won't be able to make the dessert I was planning for tonight." If the problem continues, you may want to go a step further. You could insist that your child donate some of her own money to pay for the return trip, pointing out the advantages of this solution (e.g., it compensates others for her having inconvenienced them, and it could lessen their hard feelings toward her). When she offers restitution, everyone benefits.

As when dealing with hygiene problems (see chapter 5), you could also ask your child whether next time she would rather stay home and use some of her own money to pay someone to keep her company. That way she bears some of the cost for not accommodating to the family agenda. Give her options, but also let her know that some decisions can be expensive.

Tip

If your child frequently sabotages your shopping, shop for essentials and the items *you* want first. Buy what she likes at the end. If she wants you to buy snacks, for example, say, "We can get the snacks before we leave, if we're still interested in shopping." Even if this makes your shopping trip less efficient (e.g., instead of working through the aisles in order, you pass the snack aisle at first and return to it later), her behavior may improve.

Exercise: Help Your Child Know What to Do When She's Bored (Ages 5–10)

You can make your errands together more pleasurable for your child, but they still might not be very exciting for her. The goal of this exercise is to help your child be resilient and find a way to make the best of a situation. Sometimes you will not be able to accommodate to her preferences, and it's important that she make herself comfortable. As she grows older, complaints of boredom will not get her very far. So next time you take her to do some shopping, prior to leaving, ask her, "What can you do to make the trip better for yourself?" Here are some ideas:

- *Bring along a magazine.*

- *Offer ideas about the purchase.*

- *Follow the Golden Rule. (Someday your child will be in the position of having to bring others along and will want others to cooperate.)*

- *Listen to what the clerk or salesperson is saying. (Someday your child may want to buy the very same thing.)*

Peer Relationships

Does your child criticize other children to gain a sense of superiority? Does she attempt to "buy" friends by giving away personal items, revealing low self-esteem? Does she complain of mistreatment to get you to rush to her defense? Does she often stay by herself on the playground or play only with children who are out of the popular circle? If so, you probably want this to change. You want your child to have a happy social life and feel comfortable mingling with a variety of children.

Misbehaving with Peers

Quite often when a child with ADHD encounters another rambunctious child, her behavior becomes extreme. She avoids feeling inferior when she acts silly and does not try to meet expectations, and there is no failure when she fools around with another limit tester. There is power in numbers, and your child gains momentum and clout when she teams up with a "partner in crime."

Solutions

You can try to keep your child away from other children who act out. However, this may give your child the message that she is weak and easily corrupted. Another strategy is to help her understand why she is misbehaving and help her effectively manage what happens when she encounters negative influences. This approach gives her the message that she can assert herself and produce change in her environment. She can see herself as a leader with good sense. You might say, "Maybe your friend will be smart enough to copy you when you play together."

You can also ask your child how she feels about getting in trouble and raise the concern "How do you want others to see you?" You can help her figure out what to do when others are pushing the envelope and explore whether she is afraid that others will make fun of her if she does not join in.

You might also investigate whether there is something appealing about the limit testing, because the shenanigans might be misguided ways to gain notoriety (see "Attention," in chapter 3) or ways to undermine authority (see "Antagonism"). Let your child know that solving her problematic behavior with her friends has a key benefit: it makes it fun to bring them along on family excursions.

Doubting Acceptability

When your child doubts that she is acceptable to others, it may be more difficult for her to behave reasonably. She certainly gets others to smile when she clowns around, but the unfortunate side effect is that she gets attention for immature behavior. She temporarily profits from behaviors that will not serve her well in the end. When that is the case, you might ask, "Do you feel that you have to show off or do something silly to get people to notice you?" Then ask, "How does that work for you?" If she says it works poorly, ask, "I wonder whether there are other ways to get them interested?"

You want your child to retain her great sense of humor, but you do not want her to be excessive or foolish. She has many attributes that others will enjoy, and you want her to put her best foot forward. Her ADHD behavior may decrease substantially when she is socially comfortable and secure that she is a likeable soul. Her selection of friends is also likely to change when she feels good about herself.

Nurturing Positive Social Behavior (Ages 6–10)

You can promote new friendships and mature conflict resolution by asking your child the following questions.

- "What would happen if you tried to play with someone new?"
  - "What could you do together?"
  - "What would you say to this girl?"
- "What could you do if you asked this girl to play and she said no?"
- "What could you do if she teased you or did something that you didn't like?"
- "What could you do to make things better with her?"

Supporting Social Development

If your child is on the younger side, she will likely repeat many behaviors that she learns within the family with other people. If she is demanding and possessive with you, she may also be demanding and possessive with her playmates. If family members dominate or belittle her, she may overreact or show intimidation when peers give her a hard time. For these reasons, it's important to nurture behaviors that will work well with non–family members. If you want her to share, respect social boundaries, and behave assertively with her peers, help her experience that way of interacting within the family.

When supporting her social development, it's also helpful to give your child an opportunity to interact with other children. This is how she will increase her social skill. Encourage her initiative and planning by saying "Let me know when you want to invite someone over so we can make arrangements for a playdate."

You may find that your child prefers to associate with younger children because she likes the social power or the opportunity to regress and become infantile. You may also find that she seeks older children who expose her to new things and take special care of her. But make sure she has contact with children her same age as well, because this presents more opportunities to resolve problems around sharing and competition. And she will have to relate to this age group in her classroom.

Equally important, give your child plenty of opportunity to decide what is fair and reasonable when you talk with her about her social interactions. This will prepare her to be socially effective in the future. If you notice a problem, talk with her about your concerns and help her find a good way to resolve her social dilemma. For example, you might say, "Does screaming at your friend get her to do what you want?" As with etiquette, each time she figures out a workable solution, she becomes more socially adept. Sharing is essential for social success.

Exercise: The Sharing Game (Ages 5–10)

This exercise teaches turn taking, compromising, and assertiveness. If your child is closer to five, use a set of blocks, action figures, dolls, or other related toys. If your child is closer to ten, try the same exercise with unrelated toys. This makes it more challenging to figure out a way to satisfy both of you.

Gather or show the toys to your child. Ask her, "How can we share these?" Then try out the system she proposes as you play with the toys. If you notice problems with her system, ask her to find a way that works for both of you. Then it's your turn to design a sharing system. Let her know that she can tell you if she does not like the way you are sharing.

Problems When You Visit with Others

Raising a child can be both pleasurable and difficult. When your child shows ADHD behavior, being a parent can feel overwhelming. If you are without assistance and isolated, your situation worsens considerably. You may desperately want to socialize with adult friends, but your child's behavior may make social visits seem almost impossible to manage.

If your child is accustomed to being the center of your universe, ADHD behavior probably works to keep things that way. When you are busy with something else and it's not all about her, she immediately does something to bring you back. Her ADHD behavior keeps you glued to her. If you are brave and take her on a social visit, hoping to have a few moments to relax and enjoy the company of your friend, she makes sure that you will not forget her. She makes a constant commotion. She yanks you from your conversation and interrupts. She jumps on you or makes a mess that pulls your attention away from your friend. When you ask her to clean up, she refuses. You are continuously distracted because you must keep attending to her. You feel embarrassed, and it's impossible to conduct a conversation. When she hears you mention her difficult behaviors, the problem worsens. The more she shows ADHD behavior, the more she remains the hot topic of your conversation. And if you cut your visit short, you simply reinforce her to keep behaving in the same way, because now she has you all to herself again.

Solutions

Getting your child to cooperate during social visits is not only good for you, it's good for her as well. If she is going to be successful with teachers and other people, she must learn to tolerate not being the center of attention. She must learn to accommodate to what is expected and share the spotlight. She must learn to make the best of a situation when she cannot get exactly what she wants. A social visit in another person's home requires all of these skills, so it's a great opportunity for your child to learn some mature behaviors.

Making Your Visit to Another Person's Home a Positive Experience (Ages 4–10)

First, recognize that some situations are very difficult for children, so take your child with you only if you think there is a possibility of some success. With that in mind, here are some tips to help your visit go smoothly.

- Before you leave, talk with your child about what is likely to happen during the visit. If she has objections, try to make changes that help her feel comfortable.

- Talk with her about problems that keep repeating during visits. Work out ways to handle these problems.

- Bring along something that she likes to play with.

- Help her feel welcomed and included when you arrive. Invite her to participate in the conversation, and embrace her involvement.

- Ask your host, "Would you like any help?" and see whether your child is interested in joining in.

- Compliment her in front of your host. Talk about her self-reliance and recent achievements.

- If she is interested in participating, avoid getting involved in lengthy conversations that exclude her. When you think she has something to say about a topic, solicit her input. If she wants to sit with you (even on your lap), cuddle with her so that she feels wanted. Reassure her physically (and verbally) that you enjoy being together. She does not have to talk, but this will help her feel included.

- If she eventually becomes immersed in her own activity, leave her be.

- When conversing with your host, remember that your child could be listening. Don't talk about her negative behavior, avoid making negative comments about other family members, and don't talk about private family matters. If you do, your child may resent the fact that you tell others her business and may sabotage your visit. Also, if she thinks you are upset or sad because of something you say, she may act out to distract you.

Wanting to Quit Group Activities

You probably want your child to get involved with organized groups and extracurricular activities, because you know that this helps a child's physical and social development and promotes discipline. Often, signing your child up for such things requires fees, commitments, and much effort on your part. After jumping through all of those hoops, it can be devastating to hear that your child refuses to go (see "Avoidance," in chapter 3). You may feel that quitting is not an option: you want her to recognize the importance of fulfilling obligations, develop her inner strength, and learn to deal with problems head on.

To make that happen, you may threaten your child with punishment and demand continued attendance once she has enlisted in a structured activity. After all, it's not right for anyone to break a commitment. Others are counting on her (and you) to follow through, and you do not want to let them down.

Sometimes your child may give in to your demands and keep attending. But this way of handling things may not always work out very well. She may "go through the motions" and barely try; her behavior could be an embarrassment. The situation can feel like a disaster because you want her to have a good experience, but all you get is moaning and groaning.

Solutions

You can talk with your child about the impact that her actions have on her and on team or group members who rely on her continued participation. You can also say, "If you really want to quit, then would you make the call to _____ [the coach, teacher, organizer, etc.] and say that you're quitting?" in the hope that this will motivate her to stick with the activity.

But a desire to quit can indicate that your child is disappointed with the activity. It can mean that she is overreacting to a lack of success, is hearing negative comments from the sidelines, is having social difficulty, or is fearful. It can also mean that she is punishing you (see "Antagonism," in chapter 3) or that she is feeling coerced to do the activity. Unless those problems are resolved, she will be reluctant to keep participating.

Find a Comfortable Resolution

Your initial goal is to help your child feel safe telling you what is bothering her. You might ask, "What is making it difficult for you to be there?" It may take some probing for her to open up, because some problems are difficult to admit. So don't expect her to get to the point immediately.

Sometimes the solution is relatively easy. For example, you might ask another child to tutor your child so that she can gain mastery without having to perform in front of an audience. You could encourage her to watch other children do the activity so that she can see how it's done. Or you could ask her to coach a less skillful child, which would reinforce her sense of competence.

Your child, however, may continue to resist and remain fearful. When that happens, you can break the activity into less intimidating steps and make the conditions of learning as nonthreatening as possible to help her acclimate. But let her know that if she wants to feel better, avoidance will not help her.

Exercise: Desensitize Your Child Who Wants to Quit (Ages 6–12)

Your child will be less likely to quit if you reduce her fears. In psychology, we call this *desensitizing*. You can help desensitize your child by asking her, "What would be so terrible if that happened?" You can also ask, "What could you do to make it better?" Both questions can help her calm down and adapt.

Here is an example of Karin desensitizing Alicia, and you can use the same approach with your child whenever she is fearful or overreacting.

Alicia: I'm quitting dance.

Karin: What's so awful about dancing?

Alicia: I'm the worst dancer in our group.

Karin: What's so terrible about that?

Alicia: They might not let me dance in the recital because I'm so bad.

Karin: So what could you do if you they didn't let you perform this year?

Alicia: I'd never go back.

Karin: Would that make it better?

Alicia: No.

Karin: So what else could you do?

Alicia: I could keep practicing and take more lessons to catch up.

Karin: What would be so terrible about that?

Stop Negligence

On other occasions, your child might have signed on for an activity without giving adequate thought to the commitment. She might be quitting as soon as she encounters the slightest problem, and she might be spending your money frivolously. When that is the case, you may feel it's important to set firm limits to stop the negligence. Underwriting costly activities when your child is careless is not good for either of you. So prior to signing her up again, let her know that she will have to pay a share of the fee. If she fulfills the obligation, you can always pay her back at that time. You want her to have a stake in finishing.

However, be advised: if you make it too difficult for your child to start or stop an activity, your discipline can backfire. It can increase her reluctance to try something new. You want her to remain curious and adventuresome. You do not want her to be anxious about being trapped and uncomfortable. If she cannot get out, she may not get in, and she may learn to avoid activities that could be enriching and beneficial. You do not want "commitments" to be associated with negativity.

The Next Step

We have identified new ways to help your child care for herself and cooperate both inside and outside of the house and family. But we have not yet explored ways to help her succeed in school. This is our next big step, but, given what you have already learned, you are well on your way.

8 Adjusting Your Child to School

When your child's behavior at home and his behavior at school are notably different, ask yourself: *What's dissimilar about these two settings? Why are problems occurring in one setting and not the other?* For instance, if your child has social or learning difficulties, it may be very difficult for him to adjust to school. He may show ADHD behavior that is much more severe when he is at school in comparison to when he is at home. Conversely, if he is exceedingly bright, or if the classroom structure settles him, school might be far less problematic.

Who Does the Accommodating?

Most ADHD interventions recommend that schools adjust to the needs of the child with ADHD. If the school does not make the recommended changes, parents are encouraged to pressure administrators until the adjustments occur. However, insisting that the school make all the adjustments comes with an important risk: *your child may not learn to adapt to others' ways and adjust to the world the way it is.*

Parents' beliefs about ADHD influence the direction that they take with their child's problems at school. When they believe that ADHD is a permanent biological disability, they want the school to provide a permanent accommodation. They assume that their child will always be dependent on special services. They accept that their child will always need a personal classroom attendant, a second set of books, extra time to complete work, preferred seating, and close monitoring from everyone involved.

But as you have learned throughout this book, you do not have to take that path. Your child can learn to stop showing ADHD behavior, and you can wean him from the extra help he is used to. While your child may initially benefit from special services, you can focus on identifying current weaknesses that keep him from prospering in school. You can then work diligently to reduce his need for a customized curriculum (remember principle 10: foster independence).

If you feel that your child cannot make progress without an accommodation, try to limit how long he will receive it, and also try to reduce it in a stepwise process. For example, if he could initially benefit from a classroom aid or a check-in person, ask yourself, *What does he have to learn so that he no longer needs that accommodation?*

Learning in Groups

When your child begins school, he must make a monumental adjustment from the life he is used to. He must separate from you and conform to the dictates of strangers who want full compliance. He must leave the security of one-to-one interaction and his familiar home environment to spend most of his time mixed in with many children vying for limited attention.

In any elementary classroom you can spot the children with ADHD. Just wait for the teacher to pull the class together for "whole group" instruction. Then watch who fidgets, squirms, and fails to participate. While the other children are following the teacher's instructions and listening to her presentation, a child with ADHD is often unruly, not participating, and amusing others. His antics disrupt the entire lesson. His problematic responding in groups is a serious detriment to his success in school. His teacher will worry about how his actions will affect others and her success at teaching.

The Difficulty of Groups

Groups may be difficult for your child for any of the following reasons.

- He feels excluded.

- He objects to the coercion that occurs when leaders manage groups.

- He is intimidated by the group and wishes to avoid the risk of exposing his inadequacies.

The larger the group, the worse these problems can get.

Your child must learn to defer to others to be successful in groups. He must suspend his wants, expand his interests, and be receptive to what others find important. He must share, take turns, and make a public display of his competence. If his teacher is presenting a lesson, he must submit to her full control. All of these behaviors may be difficult when his family behavior is quite the opposite.

At home, your child's actions may often run counter to the family group. When the family is together and looking for him to join, he may be busy doing his own thing. When he is uninvited, he may frequently intrude. When others have the limelight, he may shift the focus to him. The family may get used to this behavior and shrug it off, but his teacher will not. In order to thrive in group settings, your child must learn to blend in.

Solutions

Spending time alone with your child is great for building intimacy. However, it's also important that you provide him with plenty of opportunity to be part of a group. Bring the family together as a unit as often as possible, to help him learn the behaviors he will need in the classroom. When family members are engaged in activities that isolate them from one another, such as watching TV in different rooms, your child misses out on learning to interact with others and get along in groups. The only way for your child to learn how to deal effectively with people is through practice. Try to have "small group" discussions in which you bring up interesting topics and share thoughts and feelings. Ask him about events that are important to him, and find out about his day.

To develop your child's group etiquette, train him to follow and participate in a conversation shared among at least three people (see the exercise below). Normally your child may drop out of such a conversation quickly if the topic is not one that particularly interests him. Yet you can slowly teach him to pay better attention to topics that others bring up and to take turns in a discussion. The key is to make group activity a pleasure so that he wants to stay involved. You can accomplish this simply by encouraging appropriate behavior: show him that others enjoy his company and are glad he is a member of the group when he (a) builds on the conversation in understandable and relevant ways instead of shifting it off course and (b) waits patiently until others finish before speaking.

Overcoming Obstacles to Effective Group Communication (Ages 5–12)

Interrupting. To address frequent interrupting, signal your child to wait by affectionately touching his arm while you continue to speak or attend to the speaker. Later on, you can ask him, "How do we know when someone is finished speaking?" and explore the signals together. Also, resolve his fears about not getting a turn to talk.

Lack of participation. If your child is on the fringe of the conversation, kindle his participation. Look in his direction and mention something that may be significant to him. That will let him know that you welcome his involvement. You can always say, "I hope everyone feels free to join in," to emphasize that he is invited. React positively when he is willing to be part of the group and when he takes an interest in what others are saying. If it's necessary to be more direct, ask him, "Would you be willing to share some of your thoughts with us?"

Lack of clarity. If it's difficult to understand what your child is communicating, ask for clarification: "I'm not sure I got it. Would you say that again?" Letting him endlessly ramble will not help him learn to explain his thoughts. Give him the message that you are eager to learn about his ideas and observations. His sense of belonging and importance to the group will increase when there is clear communication.

Monopolizing. If your child is monopolizing the conversation, gently interrupt: "You're saying some interesting things. What's the important idea that you want us to hear?" Or kindly ask, "Would you like to see whether anyone else wants to join in?" Later on, in private, you can ask, "I wonder whether people would listen better if you got right to the point and took a shorter turn speaking?"

Lack of relevancy. If your child makes an irrelevant comment, tenderly ask, "What were we saying that got you to think of that?" or suggest, "Maybe there's a way to tie that into what we're talking about." You do not want to offend him, but you want him to stay on track. If he gets back to the main theme, respond positively and build on his comments. Encourage him to keep a discussion going rather than detract from it.

Don't forget to model acceptable group behavior yourself.

Exercise: Helping Your Child Adapt to a Group (Ages 5–12)

You can help your child operate effectively in groups by providing practice and carefully manipulating three variables: group size, the length of time that your child must listen while others speak, and the length of time spent talking about subject matter that interests others.

This exercise is meant to be repeated, with more people in the group the more you do it. Recruit friends and relatives with whom your child has a positive relationship. Ask them to read this section of the book so that they will know what you are trying to accomplish. Then follow these steps:

- *Get together as a group. The first time you do this exercise, three people is plenty.*

- *Begin a discussion. At first, talk only about what your child likes (video games, hobbies, books, etc.), and allow him to be the center of attention.*

- *Carefully, increase the time that others talk about his interests.*

147

- *Slowly, introduce other topics. Kindle his participation and seek his opinion.*

- *Gradually, reduce your efforts to keep him involved, and increase the time spent talking about the interests of others.*

As your child learns to listen and contribute when others speak about their interests, gradually increase the size of the group. If you notice problems listening and contributing, ease back on the steps and make changes more slowly.

Other Reasons for School Difficulty

Apart from problems operating in groups, there are often other reasons children diagnosed with ADHD have difficulty in school. If something is impeding your child's progress in school, it's essential that you identify as many contributing factors as you can.

Learning Difficulty

Approximately one-third of children diagnosed with ADHD show some kind of learning disability (Spencer, Biederman, and Wilens 1998). If your child has a specific learning problem, such as dyslexia (i.e., developmental reading disorder), be sure to enroll him in a specialized curriculum. Work closely with the school and perhaps a professional tutor to make sure he gets the necessary services.

But it's not surprising that children who have difficulty learning are more likely to show ADHD behavior; their probability for success is lower. Their avoidance and unruliness protect them from exposing their inadequacies. However, ADHD behavior usually makes the problem worse. Without practice, no one learns very well, and learning slows down as the focus shifts to the child's behavior.

Tip

Your child will improve in reading, writing, and arithmetic if he learns to do the following, which you can help him with at home:

- Read aloud so it sounds just like talking.

- Draw his letters and numbers exactly as shown.

- Memorize math facts (e.g., single-digit addition, subtraction, or multiplication).

Fear of Failure

A child's concern about lack of competence may trigger ADHD behavior with schoolwork. You may notice, for example, that your child neglects to write down his assignments or bring materials home, but these oversights have the powerful effect of shielding him (at least temporarily) from the difficulties and disappointments that he dreads. Playing by the rules does not result in success for him, so why follow the rules or play at all? His forgetfulness protects him from feeling like a failure.

Sometimes schoolwork may be so threatening and uncomfortable for your child that he grasps his pencil so tightly his hand hurts. He may second-guess his responses to such an extent he may lose his train of thought and beg you for the answer so that he will not commit a mistake. He may overreact, slap himself, and say that he is stupid. But that kind of frustration only harms his performance, even if it sometimes gets others to ease their expectations. Rushing through an assignment or giving up can free him from the frustrations that he encounters (see "Avoidance," in chapter 3). Not finishing, on the other hand, can help too, by delaying negative evaluation for poor task completion.

In class your child may not ask questions because he does not want to expose his ignorance. Similarly, if when he is doing homework you check in with him and offer to help, he may say impatiently, "I know, I know," so that you leave him alone. The truth is he may resent your butting in because it makes him feel pressured and implies that he is inadequate.

Solutions

If the prospect of failing disrupts your child, it's very important that you react calmly to his mistakes. He will be more tolerant of his errors if you are. Getting overly excited about small successes, however, may not help him work hard. Let him know that most of the time people have to struggle through many obstacles to succeed in meaningful ways.

Overcoming Fear of Failure (Ages 6–12)

Asking your child the following kinds of questions may help reduce his avoidance and defensiveness with schoolwork.

- "How bad does it have to get before it's worthwhile for you to try?"

- "What if you were brave and asked a question in front of others?"

- "Are you afraid to try when you see others doing well?"

- "Will something terrible happen if it's challenging and you have to struggle?

- "Maybe there's a way to figure out the hard part?"

- "What will happen if you make a mistake or admit you're wrong?"

- "What could you do if you have trouble understanding?"

- "Will you be happier if you don't try?"

- "Maybe we can figure out why the mistakes are happening?"

- "What are you saying no to?"

- "What will help you feel more at ease?"

- "What if you pretend it's just like building a model?"

- "Is there anything good about making mistakes?"

The Benefits of Dependency

There is security and power in your child's dependency on you. By behaving in ways that activate your protective instincts, he can avoid venturing into the unknown and have you take care of problems for him. For many children with ADHD, relationships are all about getting relief from problems. However, this leaves precious little time to enjoy each other's company in more mature ways.

Because school can be your child's first experience away from you, it can ignite problems with separation, abandonment, and dependency for both of you. While he may expect the same nurturing at school that you give him at home, that same amount of attention is impossible in a classroom of twenty-five students. If he complains that he does not get enough individual time at home, he may feel even more deprived at school. He may want to leave school or have you come and get him.

Your child's problems at school can be a way to make sure you do not forget about him. Problems can draw you in like a magnet. Have you ever had to leave work when you got a call from school that your child was acting out? He seems unaware of the consequences of his actions, but you come to his rescue, pick up the pieces, give him a pep talk, and perhaps defend him. These benefits are difficult for him to give up, and they can consume the entire family (see "Attention," in chapter 3).

It's common, however, for parents to worry that others will blame them for not doing enough, so they do even more. They go to great lengths to keep harmful school consequences from occurring. They end up doing much of their child's homework after they hear his complaints and threats to give up. While the unfinished work and procrastination frighten them, their efforts to salvage his grades do very little to develop his academic skill or autonomy.

Social Problems

Everyone likes to be part of a team when they are in the starting lineup. But what happens with the benched players? If your child is struggling academically or socially and does not blend in, he becomes like a player at the far end of the bench. His enthusiasm and immersion in what is happening is likely to fade, just as with the player who never gets into the game.

If your child is not getting along with teachers or peers, he may feel uncomfortable and even quite alienated. This may increase his desire to escape and disrupt, and he may have difficulty enduring the school day. These kinds of problems can intensify during adolescence, when social relationships become even more important.

• Noah's Story

Noah, a fourth-grader, came home from school with a report listing several transgressions that had occurred over the course of the day: he called out in class instead of raising his hand, he talked excessively, he grabbed a pencil from another student (Ethan), and he ran down the hall loudly on the way to recess. Problems were compounding because of his frequent overreacting. His extreme behavior made it difficult for teachers and peers to get along with him.

For a long time, school personnel had told Noah's parents that he had problems "controlling" himself. They described him as "impulsive," and they used the word "disinhibited" during team meetings. It sounded as if Noah could not stop himself from behaving inappropriately because he had ADHD. They suggested that Noah's parents use stringent discipline to offset his disability.

In the past, Noah's parents had complied with that recommendation. However, this time, they wanted to resolve the trouble in a different way. They wanted to use a nonthreatening approach that would allow Noah to explore better ways of handling the problems he was encountering. They were not interested in stopping the school from taking away his recess, because that was school policy. But they did want to redirect him to a more constructive solution without distracting him with more negativity.

First, they invited Noah to talk about what happened at school. Because Noah knew that they had been patient with him over the past months, it was easy for him to tell them about the unfortunate events that had taken place. Noah's parents were glad that he was comfortable talking to them, and they listened to his story without evaluating or judging what he was saying. They wanted to work as a team, and Noah responded very well to their invitation to speak frankly.

Instead of seeing the pencil-grabbing incident as a "disinhibited" act, his parents asked him, "What was going on with you and Ethan when you grabbed the pencil?" They knew it was important to investigate Noah's relationship with his classmate, and they learned that the pencil grabbing was retaliation. Noah had allowed Ethan to borrow his pencil, and when Ethan teased him later in the day, he felt betrayed. Noah often endured ridicule from other classmates, and now his feelings were hurt and he was upset. He knew that grabbing the pencil was wrong, but he lashed out, just like many people do when frustrations build and problems accumulate.

Noah's parents then asked him whether his angry responses were getting him what he wanted. They recognized that pressuring him to give up the retaliating was unlikely to work very well unless he wanted to make a change. They thought that Noah was more likely to try something new if he announced that his grabbing solution was not working *for him*.

Once his parents felt that he was open to changing, they empathetically said, "Ethan's behavior must have been hard on you." They then asked, "How do you want to handle the teasing next time?" Because he had to live with the consequences, it was important that he endorse the solutions. Their goal was to assist him in figuring out options that might work better.

After discussing various possibilities, Noah decided that it was a good idea to talk with Ethan rather than keep the fight going. His parents then asked, "What will you do if Ethan still reacts negatively?" because they wanted to desensitize him to what he feared (see chapter 7). Thankfully, things worked out well with Ethan, and this encouraged Noah to use talking as a solution later in the week with another child.

Noah's parents also found out that his running loudly down the hall had occurred after his teacher criticized him in front of the entire class. When it was time for recess, he bolted to the play yard because it felt good to escape. Unfortunately, and similar to the pencil-grabbing incident, his hotheaded response had serious side effects. It did nothing to enhance his relationship with his teacher or school administrators.

As a way to remedy this problem, Noah's parents asked him whether he would like to repeat the talking solution with his teacher. They asked, "Would it work out better for you if you told your teacher what was bothering you when the class takes a break?" They also explored the possibility of scheduling a meeting with his teacher when Noah doubted that his teacher would listen to him.

Overall, Noah's parents had a very definite goal. They wanted to help him substitute the physical manifestation of discontentment with verbal peacemaking. With enough repetition and success, they anticipated that this new way of responding would become his new habit. They knew that once it became a habit, he would not have to think of doing it before he responded. He would simply react in this new socially acceptable way when encountering similar situations in the future. This is how Noah's parents helped him stop his "out of control" behavior.

Developing the Desire to Achieve

Your child may cram his schoolwork into his backpack as if it were garbage, relying on you to sift through his papers, discover notes from his teachers, and find assignments. For him, it's "out of sight, out of mind." You end up reminding him about all the work he has not yet finished. He tells you he will do it later, but later never comes. You pressure him to achieve, and he does everything possible to squirm away.

So what can you do to help your child overcome his concerns about failure, separation, and social acceptability? What approach will help him complete schoolwork independently and enjoy his time at school? Forcing obedience or rescuing him may get him to the next grade, but what will help him become a serious student who wants to achieve on his own?

Resolving Problems with Schoolwork

If you have already started nurturing your child's self-management, you have been encouraging your child to complete household and self-care tasks more independently. His schoolwork fits into the same framework. You want him to feel that school is an opportunity, not a burden.

Helping Your Child Succeed in School (Ages 6–12)

You can facilitate independent school adjustment and achievement with the following questions and comments applicable to the situation. As always, use a positive tone of voice with your child. Help him resolve problems in ways that make sense to him; don't use coercion or "twist his arm."

- "What's stopping you from wanting to go to school? What's wrong?"

- "Would you like to find a way to get your work done and still have time to play?"

- "Do you like school more when you stare at the clock?" (playful tone)

- "What can you do so that you aren't bored? Would you like to talk with your teacher about ways to make the class interesting?"

- "What study system works best for you? Would you like to make any changes?"

- "We know you learn a lot from your video games. I wonder whether some of those skills could help you with your schoolwork."

- "Would you like to find a way to get the correct assignment?"

- "What don't you like about your teacher? Does he remind you of someone else you're angry with?"

- "How do you want it to go with your teacher?"

- "What can you do to get that to happen?"

- "Will disrupting the class or embarrassing her solve the problem?"

- "Will something bad happen if you let the teacher tell you what to do?"

- "Sometimes I wonder whether you'd rather stay with the principal (or nurse). Is it better than cooperating with your teacher?"

- "I'm noticing that you're not doing your homework."

  - "Are you sure that you want to do that to yourself?"

  - "I wonder why you feel so negative about it."

- "Does it feel like you're doing me a favor when you finish your work? Will *you* feel better if you complete it and check for mistakes?

- "Your teacher is going to keep you in for recess if you don't pass in your homework. Is that okay with you?"

- "If you daydream or refuse to do your work, you'll fall behind. Is it worth it to you?"

- "If you start late, you'll have less time to fix problems if anything goes wrong. It might be too late for me or anyone else to help. Do you want to put yourself in that position?"

- "This might be a good time to finish your schoolwork. We're going out later."

- "Would you like to figure a way to stay on track and succeed?"

  - "What if your friends call while you're doing homework?"

  - "How much work do you want to finish before you stop?"

  - "What can you do to take care of yourself if your friends misbehave in class?"

  - "What if you waited until recess to socialize?"

- "We can pay for summer *school* or summer *camp*." (playful tone) "I guess it's up to you."

- "Who are you punishing when you don't do your work?" (playful tone)

  - "I know you're angry, but what kind of student do you want to be?"

  - "Do you want to let this problem keep you from achieving the way you want?"

Students Have a Privileged Status

Children often resent school because they feel that they are forced to do work without getting anything in return. To them, being a student means being enslaved. This way of thinking becomes so extreme that some adolescents would rather drop out and get a menial job than continue being a student.

You can counteract this mind-set by teaching your child that being a student is a privileged status. Let him know that others will inconvenience themselves to promote his success at school. Show him that the family will organize schedules and subsidize any family member who is interested in being serious about academics. Let him know that knowledge confers special value and importance to the family (and to society). Finally, emphasize that while success at school may lead to a lucrative job, education has a value of its own, and the school experience itself can be very enjoyable.

Ways to Emphasize the Value of Being a Student (Ages 6–12)

Following are some ways you can communicate the importance of your child's education to you and your family. Note that taking action to support your child's success and being willing to participate or listen are essential to this approach.

- "We can set aside extra money to help you with your learning."

- "Shall I pick you up later so you can work with your teacher after school?"

- "You've been working hard in school all week. Sure I can make time to give you a ride."

- "It's a pleasure helping out a serious student."

- "I know you're interested in spaceships. I saw this book about them at the store and bought it for you."

- "I'm willing to set aside time in the evening to work together. I can start as early as you want."

- "The more you learn, the more you can teach us about what you know."

- "You're becoming very knowledgeable."

- "It's very impressive when you do that."

- "You'll be able to hire a lot of people to work for you in the future."

- "Your mother would love it if you told her about the dinosaur book you're reading at the family meal tonight."

The Homework Crisis

ADHD specialists doubt the accuracy of an ADHD diagnosis if problems with homework are not occurring (Murphy and Gordon 1998). This is not surprising. Homework brings together all the conditions that trigger ADHD behavior for most children.

Homework, for a child, represents an extreme conflict of interest. The activity demands exceptional accommodation to others. The child must do schoolwork when not in school. He must come home from a work setting and, instead of playing, do more work. Seldom will a child feel more imposed on. How many children have ever asked for homework?

It's not surprising if your child does not want to take time to read directions or check his work, or that he sneaks, lies, and avoids when homework is on the agenda. In fact, some children feel so upset by homework that they would rather fail (by not doing it) than submit to the perceived oppression. However, for other children, a reluctance to do homework represents an avoidance of responsibility or a veiled attempt to keep loved ones involved and attentive (Bruns 1993).

A Common Response

While some parents are squeamish about making their child do homework because it interferes with other activities, there is often close monitoring of homework in many families. Those parents perceive homework completion as a necessary ingredient for their child's success. Many end up badgering their child to start the assignment as soon as the child enters the house. The assignment becomes a nightmare that he wants to escape. He may protest by taking hours to finish only one or two problems, and these power struggles can monopolize the entire evening. There can be tremendous negativity surrounding even the smallest homework assignment.

Increase Your Child's Control

Your child may tolerate homework better if he has more say over what happens. So instead of determining when, where, and how he does his

159

assignments, find out what arrangement is preferable to him (principle 8: establish "buy in").

For example, some children dislike segregation when they work. It may be helpful to allow your child to do his work in a common area, such as the dining room. Other children like to have music or the TV on in the background. See whether that helps, and revisit the problem if it does not (principle 4: be patient).

Allowing your child to create his own environment may also help make homework less troublesome. If he *wants* to get it done, he will find a way to do it. You know that he is very good at tuning out distractions when he is intent on finishing what he is doing. When he is "on a mission," even a loud voice may fail to unglue him.

There are plenty of opportunities for your child to both do homework and play. Taking away playtime until he does his homework may make him resent the assignments even more. As with many other coerced activities, if he thinks he is being hassled, he will lose momentum, and the faintest sound could throw him off task.

Tip

Often children feel controlled as soon as a parent asks them whether they have any homework. Let your child know that you are asking this question merely to coordinate your schedules. You are simply taking an interest in his life.

Develop a Routine

If you establish a daily homework routine, it's more likely that your child will complete his homework smoothly. Like a sleep response, his body will get a work response at a particular time. This happens with basketball players when they develop a consistent way to shoot free throws, and your child could get a similar benefit as well.

Build Independence

If your child is very young, begin by doing the assignment together during a special quiet time that happens on a consistent basis. Keep him company and resolve any problems that threaten to overwhelm him. Later, promote his self-management by allowing him to stay in the lead while the assignment is completed. Remember, you are facilitating; you are not doing the assignment for him. For example, you might request his opinion about what to do first when starting the assignment, and check whether he agrees with any suggestions that you make before proceeding. This reassures him that you respect his ideas and see him as competent.

The more your child takes charge, the more independence he will develop. Once he gets the knack of what to do on his own, you can shift into a parallel activity during homework time. This brings you a step closer to independent homework completion. You might say, "How about I do my house bills while you complete some of these school items?" Eventually, you inch away, and he completes his home studies without you. Let him know that his independence allows you to finish other tasks and gives you more time to play together later on.

Give It a Positive Twist

You can help make homework more meaningful and positive for your child by reframing it as an opportunity to practice. Tell him that just as athletes train between games or events, homework is like training for schoolwork. Because there is usually not enough time during school to master new material or show his teacher all that he can do, homework can be a chance for him to develop or sharpen his skills so that he can shine in school.

Resolve Procrastination

If your child has left work undone and would rather play, snack, make a telephone call, or watch TV even when it's getting late, it's important to identify possible reasons for his delay tactics. Rather than withhold privileges until the work is finished, help him resolve his procrastinating. For instance, he may not think he can do the assignment very well, or something special might be happening in his life that is whisking him away. There might be numerous reasons that he pushes his work to the side, and it's important that you identify what reinforces the behavior. Following are some typical advantages to procrastinating:

- It creates time to focus on more pressing problems.

- It creates time to play and explore fantasies.

- It creates time to avoid work discomfort and evaluation.

- It means that any failures are due to last-minute rushing, not incompetence.

- It delays other expectations and limits (e.g., bedtime).

- There are fewer competing activities later in the evening.

- Achievements just before the deadline are more exciting and worth the effort.

- Others show concern, help more, and reduce expectations when time is short and problems grow larger.

- Delaying what others want increases social power and authority.

- When there is no investment, there is no disappointment.

After you figure out what is contributing to your child's procrastinating, discuss the advantages of completing work at an earlier time. For example, if he finishes assignments long before his bedtime, he can relax without having work hanging over his head. He may also feel less rushed and stressed when he is not working until the last possible moment. Yes, it might be less thrilling, but it's less nerve-racking when he can take his time and work at a comfortable pace. He might even find that he is more pleased with the results. You can also point out that if he comes to you for consultation, you can do a better job when you are not tired and rushed. Your interactions are likely to be more pleasurable when you work together at an earlier time. However, it's also important to model the behavior you want him to do. Accept your responsibility to do assigned tasks at home without procrastinating as well.

Passing in Assignments

There is yet another major concern regarding the homework crisis. Many children diagnosed with ADHD often do not pass in their assignments even though they completed the work the night before. Why does this happen?

First, if your child is accustomed to having others remind him to put on his coat, brush his teeth, and get his backpack, why is it surprising if he does not take out his assignment and pass it in when arriving at school? If his teacher does not explicitly ask him to pass in his work, it's "out of sight, out of mind."

As a way to remedy this problem, encourage your child to figure out how he will remember to give his teacher the completed assignment. Help him identify the environmental signal that will trigger him to turn in his work. This is a good time to help him figure out a "plan for success" that he can execute on his own.

There may, however, be other reasons for your child's failure to pass in assignments. He might not have done a commendable job. He could be avoiding a poor grade by not showing his teacher his work. After all, completing the assignment and forgetting to pass it in is more acceptable than handing in something terrible or not doing the work at all. Another possibility (apart from keeping you worried about his forgetfulness) is that your child is angry with you. If you fret about his grades, not passing in the assignment can be a powerful weapon to use against you (see "Antagonism," in chapter 3). But as with other spiteful responses, nothing good comes of it in the end.

Relating to Teachers

You can facilitate your child's success at school when you have a good working relationship with his teacher. But relations may be strained if you think his teacher is ineffective or if his teacher, conversely, believes you are not doing a good job parenting. This may happen if communication between you is lacking. So how do you develop a rapport with your child's teacher?

Daily Reports

Term report cards have been with us for many years. However, it's now common to monitor children diagnosed with ADHD using daily reports (Robin 2006). Daily reports have gained widespread acceptance because they have some very clear advantages. It can be very helpful to know what has happened during your child's day at school. This information enables you to quickly address problems, stopping them before they get worse.

Problems with Daily Reports

Daily reporting can be problematic when teachers frequently draw parents into problems that could be solved effectively during the school day. Many parents become distressed when problems at school spill into the evening hours. Those problems then monopolize family time, and parents dread each report.

The monitoring system can also force you into being a referee. Your child is likely to portray events at school in ways that keep him in a favorable light, while his teacher is likely to indicate that something very different occurred. Under these circumstances, if you blame your child when you did not see what happened, you can put a strain on your relationship with him. On the other hand, if you side with your child, you risk undermining his teacher's credibility. You could unfortunately encourage future noncooperative behaviors when you take a stance against his teacher. Your child may get the message that his teacher behaves incorrectly, and he may question whether it makes sense to listen to her at all. On top of that, if your child has often felt chastised at home, he may like the fact that you are now advocating for him rather than blaming him. He may keep creating drama at school because he enjoys your support. As you can see, upheaval with the teacher introduces the same kinds of problems as in family triangles (see chapter 6).

So beware: daily reports can be fraught with problems. This is very apparent when your child's access to resources at home depends on these reports. You may end up making stern rulings as soon as your child walks in the door. You may become the judge and jury, and your home life may begin to feel like a courtroom. These interactions will disrupt your relationship with your child and make matters worse.

Solutions

You can avoid these kinds of problems by changing the meaning of the daily reports. Rather than understanding the reports as forcing you to "inspect" and "pass judgment," view them as permitting you to "share" what happened during the day with your child. They can help you celebrate his successes and address problems together. They enable you to keep up with his life and maintain a constructive and intimate relationship with him.

You do not want the daily reports to put your child on the defensive. You do not want him to hide the reports or become anxious about them. If you see he has done something unacceptable, ask him, "What was happening when you reacted in that way?" and together, figure out what he wants to do to resolve the problem. If a response to his teacher is necessary, ask him whether he wants to help write the reply. If he complains that his teacher behaved poorly, ask him, "What led up to that?" Help him understand possible reasons for his teacher's actions, and help him figure out a way to make the best of the situation even if his teacher did not seem to handle things very well. No matter what, it's important that he maintain his progress in school even if circumstances are difficult with his teacher. Ask him, "How are you going to get your teacher to change?" to emphasize that it's advantageous that he make an adjustment himself.

Tip

If your child avoids talking with you about the daily reports, that should be your biggest concern. You will not have a meaningful resolution to his problems if he is hesitant to work with you and share information. You want him to seek your input and inform you about the ups and downs of his day without fear. You want him to return to school with optimism and feel that he has the tools to succeed.

Signatures

If the school requires you to sign your child's work, you have yet another problem. You do not want him to feel that others lack trust in him. You do not want him to think that you and his teacher view signatures as necessary to keep him honest.

So when you notice that your child has not completed all of his assignment, you might say, "This doesn't seem to match up; what do you think?" You do not want your child to feel belittled or that he is under surveillance like a suspected criminal. Say to him, "Your teacher asked all the parents to look over the homework assignments and sign them, and I'm happy to cooperate."

Let your child know that the request to obtain signatures and the requirement to review his work are ways to reassure him that everyone is "on the same page." The signature tells him that he has accurately fulfilled what his teacher wants him to do. It can put him at ease. The process also allows you to keep up with what he is learning so that you can provide him with better consultation if he comes to you for help later on.

Parent-Teacher Conferences

When you talk with your child's teacher, let her know you appreciate her effort. Recognize that her job is very difficult, and accept the fact that she may not be able to do exactly what you want because there are many children in the classroom. Avoid blaming her or, conversely, accepting blame for your child's problems.

It's important to share what you know: inform the teacher about what helps your child achieve and cooperate at home. Many of the strategies that you have been using at home will also work at school. Encourage her to develop your child's self-reliance and cooperation in the classroom, just as you are doing within the family. Talk with her about his sensitivities so that she will understand his overreactions, and, together, explore ways to resolve those problems. For example, if your child is anxious about exposing his inadequacies, perhaps she can highlight his successes and ask him to tutor another child when she notices that he is adept with certain topics.

It's also helpful to find out how your child is getting along with all of his teachers, classmates, and other school personnel. The information you acquire will be useful when helping him resolve problems that come to your attention as the year unfolds. Remember, he will likely show more consistency in his achievement and classroom behavior when you help him maintain positive relationships at school.

Let the teacher know about your child's interests so that she can introduce lessons that will increase his participation. Your child's alliance with his teacher is likely to improve when he knows she is actively considering him. For example, if he is a wrestling fanatic, he may be very pleased with her when she gives an assignment about a professional wrestler.

Tip

Inform your child's teacher that you keep up with the information that she sends home. Let her know that you have been working hard to resolve the ongoing problems she has identified. Your enthusiasm about your child's school progress and appreciation of the feedback will likely encourage your teacher to continue the helpful behavior.

The Next Step

We are almost finished. The next step is to identify some complications that may occur when you nurture your child's self-reliance and cooperation. You can get significant benefits when you clear these last hurdles.

9 Two Important Obstacles You May Face

The style of parenting this book recommends may be unfamiliar to you and sometimes difficult to put into practice. It may feel strange to follow these new guidelines for your own behavior; however, your comfort with them will increase the more you apply them, and soon, interacting with your child in ways that nurture her cooperation and self-reliance will become a habit.

You are likely, however, to encounter two basic obstacles when you try to develop your child's self-management. This chapter helps you identify those barriers so that you can overcome them. This final touch will make it easier for you to get the results you want.

The Way You Have Learned to Behave

The first obstacle you may encounter has to do with your own behavior. You probably had some good reasons for the way you behaved toward your child in the past. Now, however, you may be stuck in a pattern of interaction with your child that is slowing down the progress that you want to make. If so, don't blame yourself; there is nothing wrong with you. You and your child are responding to each other, and the very same parenting behavior could influence another child very differently. Yet it's important to identify your part in what is happening and get it to stop.

The table below lists some of the counterproductive interactions that parents and children with ADHD often get into. Perhaps you will see yourself and your child in one or more of these interactions. If you do, focus on making changes. In some cases, your behavior may be very difficult to alter, and it may be necessary to enlist the help of a professional counselor. It's usually very difficult for anyone to modify behaviors, so go easy on the self-criticism.

Parent behavior	Child behavior
You are anxious that your child does not like you.	She reacts negatively until she gets her way. Instead of being grateful, she expects more.
You worry a lot about what others think.	Your child gains control by embarrassing you.
You do the all the managing.	Unless you remind your child, there is rarely follow-through; she lacks self-discipline and takes you for granted.
You comment on your child's negative behavior.	She repeats the behaviors that you notice.
You overreact when your child disrespects or ignores you.	She knows she can incite you by doing those behaviors.
You work hard to settle your child.	She is irritable, is unruly, and does not self-soothe.
You hide from family chaos.	Your child creates an uproar that gets you involved.
You overly please your child to compensate for the absence of her other parent.	She expects accommodation and complains.
You make sure your child does not feel deprived.	She does not work very hard.
Your child's grandparents undermine your parenting and dote on her.	She is entitled, noncompliant, and self-centered.
You doubt yourself.	Your child dominates you.
You do not want to copy your controlling parents.	Your child takes advantage of you. She is silly, boisterous, and wild.

You get anxious when you do not stop problems immediately.	Your child receives negative attention and misses opportunities to self-manage.
You pick up after others and do not give voice to your wants.	Your child treats you like a servant.
You want someone to need you. You are lonely without your child.	She is overly dependent on you.
You dread conflict.	Your child overreacts when she does not get her way.
You are busy.	Your child's behavior is extreme; "the squeaky wheel gets the grease."
You are frequently displeased.	Your child feels inadequate, gives up easily, and stays away.
You frequently bail your child out.	She disregards potential negative consequences and indulges herself.
You go through your child's belongings to check on her.	She oversteps boundaries and frequently sneaks.
One parent gives in to make your child happy. The other parent is critical and demanding in order to make her responsible.	She underachieves and avoids.
You feel bad about your parenting.	Your child provokes and blames you. She acts victimized when you set limits.
You worry and are very protective.	Your child acts out your worst fears.
You do not organize very well.	Your child does not organize very well.
You overreact to mistakes.	Your child is reluctant either to try or to admit wrongdoing.
You blame others and side with your child.	She resists authority and complains that others mistreat her.
You are domineering.	Your child is not assertive and often avoids you.
You procrastinate.	Your child procrastinates.

You want your child to know that you are smart and talented.	She doubts herself.
You do not rest if work is unfinished.	Your child rejects your lifestyle and rests a lot. She feels neglected.
You rush to get things done.	Your child resists transitions; she has problems settling down and adjusting.
You do not want to disappoint your child.	She expects you to give in.
You nag, nitpick, and are very particular.	Your child twitches, fidgets, screams in frustration, and tries to escape.
You get involved when your child has conflict with other family members.	She provokes other family members.
You go on and on when you speak.	Your child tunes you out.
You acquiesce in order to stop problems.	Your child controls you with negative behavior.
You pamper your child.	She is immature in behavior and speech.
You keep things equal so no one feels slighted.	Your child complains and bickers when others get more.
You schedule many organized activities.	Your child protests and wants more free time.
You do not want your child to be uncomfortable.	Little inconveniences bother her.
You inconsistently ignore certain behaviors.	Your child keeps repeating a behavior until you respond.
You feel exploited by the lack of help.	Your child faults you for complaining.
You constantly correct and reprimand your child in social situations.	She receives a lot of negative attention and distracts you from interacting with others.
You tell your child that she would do great if she would only try.	She becomes more afraid to try.

If one or more of these profiles seems to fit, take a moment to figure out the possible reasons for the way you feel and interact with your child. Of course, your intentions are good, and self-reflection is difficult. However, once you identify what to change, your goal to nurture self-reliance and cooperation will be easier to achieve.

The Influence of Your Childhood

Your experiences in childhood can influence your parenting behaviors. For example, if you had a demanding and critical parent, it may be difficult to remain calm when your child behaves in that fashion. The last thing you want is to live with another person who tells you that you are not good enough. Your history with your parent makes it difficult to handle your child's hostility effectively, because when you are aggravated, you usually escalate the problem.

Your emotional responses and insecurities can affect many of your interactions with your child. For example, when you question your adequacy or believe that you have failed throughout your life, your child's floundering may remind you of your own shortcomings. Now you feel as though you are failing as a parent. If you become desperate and micromanage in order to stop the landslide, you are unlikely to be successful. Your child may dislike your frequent directing and impatience and think that you doubt her ability to achieve on her own. That could tarnish her view of herself, make her irritable, and burden her with the same self-doubt that plagues you.

Repeating Childhood Behaviors

You may also be repeating behaviors with your child that you did with your parents, because that is what is familiar to you. For example, if you were nervous about your parents' reactions and went to great lengths to keep them from getting upset, you may often respond in the same way with your child. Even parents who appear domineering or depressed may frequently lapse into these kinds of extreme responses.

People's apprehension about parental disapproval can often result in excessive pleasing when they have a child of their own. When you are concerned about a loved one blaming you or being dissatisfied, you may do whatever it takes to prevent that from happening. But regrettably, your child may not learn to be responsible or work very hard for others if you continuously labor to keep her comfortable and content (remember Jack's Story in chapter 3).

Doing the Opposite of Your Parents

You may feel that you turned out all right, and you may admire and want to copy many of your parents' behaviors. But what if you feel that your parents made mistakes in raising you? When that is the case, you may compensate by going to the opposite extreme with your own child.

But, unfortunately, you could end up with the opposite problems. For example, if you did not get enough support or attention from your parents, you may focus a great deal on your child. However, she may get accustomed to your constant attentiveness and have difficulty when she is not the centerpiece of your concerns.

Solutions

To change behaviors influenced by your childhood, it may be necessary to confront difficult subject matter. You will have to take a close look at the relationship you had with your parents, and this may include examining your fears about disapproval and loss. It may include determining whether you learned to give in, avoid, overextend, or rely on others, and whether you learned to get into heated emotional exchanges.

But it can be comforting to know that you can alter the way you interact with your child. You can recognize the influence of your childhood experiences and forge a new path. Remember, in comparison to childhood, you now have increased wherewithal and new ways to solve the problems you face.

Exercise: Change Repeating Behaviors Learned in Childhood (Parents Only)

You can better change your old behaviors when you take the time to analyze and understand them thoroughly. For this exercise, you may want to use a journal or notebook or just a piece of paper.

First, identify a frequent current behavior of yours that began in childhood. Then answer the following questions:

- What happened when you did the behavior during childhood?

- What happens now when you repeat the behavior with your child?

- Does the behavior help your child learn to be more self-reliant and cooperative? If not, what can you do instead?

Following is an example.

- *Behavior*

  I keep my problems to myself because I felt that my parents were unwilling to consider my point of view.

- *What happened when I did the behavior in childhood?*

  I spent a lot of time in my room doing solitary activities. I conformed in order to avoid conflict.

- *What happens now when I repeat the behavior with my child?*

  She behaves immaturely and creates problems to get my attention. She disregards my feelings because I don't make them known to her. I give in so that she won't create a scene.

- *Does the behavior help my child learn to be more self-reliant and cooperative? If not, what can I do instead?*

  No. I can give her more opportunity to learn social boundaries and consider the perspective of others. For example, instead of withdrawing and sacrificing my wishes, I can let her know what bothers me. I can remain assertive until I reach a compromise, and I can keep addressing the problem until I establish a routine that is acceptable to both of us.

Social Pressure

Your second obstacle is social pressure. When your child is having inter-personal and academic problems, you may feel that you must act quickly. Your landlord might be threatening to evict you because of the noise. School personnel might be notifying you that they are considering grade retention or placement in a behavior-disordered classroom. Your family might be refusing to help you with child care, and you might be getting criticism from a variety of sources.

Because many professionals (and our culture in general) advise the use of rewards, punishments, and medications, there can be intense social pressure for you to use these strategies to address the crisis at hand. You may see other parents setting up behavioral charts and giving their child a stimulant drug in the morning. You may see stories in the media that highlight improvements for those who follow conventional treatments. Often there is an instant benefit when you medicate a child or dangle a reward or punishment in front of her. Speedy results, ease of use, and widespread endorsement often tip the scales toward traditional ways to diminish ADHD behavior.

The pressure can be extreme. If you show reluctance to embrace these accepted remedies, you could face criticism. People "in the know" may think that you are neglecting the facts. They may push you to start the more popular interventions and want you to take advantage of all the accommodations that others have worked so hard to put in place for children with ADHD.

Because your child's ongoing failures could have devastating consequences, it may be scary not to submit to popular advice. Disrupted family relationships and the threat of failure in school can be demoralizing. No one wants to subject a child to such harms when people are promising quick relief.

Making a Choice

There are pros and cons to the different ways to reduce ADHD behavior, and you must weigh the risks you are willing to take. You must also decide how long you are willing to try a particular approach before you abandon it. But don't always assume that it will take too much time to nurture self-reliance and cooperation. Some parents report progress soon after they start.

Just know that commonly used ADHD treatments are short-term fixes with some long-term downsides. It will likely take time and effort for you to learn how to nurture your child's self-reliance and cooperation and for your child to recognize the benefits. Know from the start: change is not always instant when you abandon the more dominating forms of discipline.

Wrapping Up

The solution this book offers is not about controlling your child more often. Nor is it about catering to her. It's about developing her self-care and her concern for others. You are establishing a mutually respectful relationship in which obtaining her endorsement is more valuable than ordering her around. So stay calm, enjoy her company, and use a reasonable tone of voice. Communicate to her, "We're in this together, so let's solve it together."

Your child may not like having increased responsibility at first, but she will enjoy having more say over what happens in the end. She may also like the fact that she is achieving and that others appreciate what she has to offer. Yes, what she wants is important, but it's also important that she care for others and contribute to their well-being. Your job is to help her strike that key balance, because it presents the best opportunity for her future happiness.

Resources

Learning and ADHD

Visit the author's website: www.craigwiener.com.

Pros and Cons of ADHD Medications

Breggin, Peter R. 2001. *Talking Back to Ritalin: What Doctors Aren't Telling You about Stimulants and ADHD*. Rev. ed. New York: De Capo Press.

Diller, Lawrence H. 2011. *Remembering Ritalin: A Doctor and Generation Rx Reflect on Life and Psychiatric Drugs*. New York: Perigee Trade.

Communicating Effectively

Elgin, Suzette Haden. 1996. *The Gentle Art of Communicating with Kids*. New York: John Wiley & Sons.

Rosenberg, Marshall B. 2003. *Nonviolent Communication: A Language of Life*. Encinitas, CA: PuddleDancer Press.

Developing Cooperation

Chapman, Gary, and Ross Campbell. 1997. *The Five Love Languages of Children*. Chicago: Moody Publishing.

Glasser, Howard, and Jennifer Easley. 1998. *Transforming the Difficult Child: The Nurtured Heart Approach*. Arizona: Center for the Difficult Child Publications.

Developing Your Child's Self-Reliance

Glenn, H. Stephen, and Jane Nelsen. 2000. *Raising Self-Reliant Children in a Self-Indulgent World: Seven Building Blocks for Developing Capable Young People*. New York: Three Rivers Press.

Leman, Kevin. 1984. *Making Children Mind without Losing Yours*. New York: Dell Publishing.

Shure, Myrna B. (with Theresa Foy DiGeronimo). 1994. *Raising a Thinking Child: Help Your Young Child to Resolve Everyday Conflicts and Get Along with Others*. New York: Pocket Books.

Parenting Groups

Visit the website of Kathryn Kvols, founder and president of both INCAF (the International Network of Children and Families) and RCB (Redirecting Children's Behavior), at incaf.com.

The Montessori Method

The Montessori Method is a way of educating young children. It promotes self-direction, independence, concentration, and personal growth. Visit the website of a Montessori school at pincushion.com.

References

Akinbami, L. J., X. M. Liu, P. N. Pastor, and C. A. Reuben. 2011. "Attention Deficit Hyperactivity Disorder among Children Aged 5–17 Years in the United States, 1998–2009." NCHS Data Brief No. 70. August. http://www.cdc.gov/nchs/data/databriefs/db70.pdf. Aug. 18, 2011

American Psychiatric Association. 2000. *Diagnostic and Statistical Manual of Mental Disorders*. 4th ed., text revision. Washington, DC: American Psychiatric Association.

Aronen, E. T., E. J. Paavonen, M. Fjällberg, M. Soininen, and J. Törrönen. 2000. "Sleep and Psychiatric Symptoms in School-Age Children." *Journal of the American Academy of Child and Adolescent Psychiatry* 39: 502–8.

Barkley, R. A. 1998. *Attention Deficit Hyperactive Disorder: A Handbook for Diagnosis and Treatment*. 2nd ed. New York: Guilford Press.

———. 2006. *Attention Deficit Hyperactive Disorder: A Handbook for Diagnosis and Treatment*. 3rd ed. New York: Guilford Press.

———. 2009. "Deficient Emotional Self-Regulation Is a Core Symptom of ADHD." *Journal of ADHD and Related Disorders* 1: 5–37.

Barkley, R. A., K. R. Murphy, and M. Fischer. 2008. *ADHD in Adults: What the Science Says*. New York: Guilford Press.

Bruns, J. H. 1993. *They Can but They Don't: Helping Students Overcome Work Inhibition*. New York: Viking Press.

Douglas, V. I. 1972. "Stop, Look, and Listen: The Problem of Sustained Attention and Impulse Control in Hyperactive and Normal Children." *Canadian Journal of Behavioural Science* 4: 259–82.

Faraone, S. V., and A. E. Doyle. 2001. "The Nature and Heritability of Attention Deficit Hyperactivity Disorder." Child and Adolescent Psychiatric Clinics of North America 10: 299–316.

Ferber, R. 1985. *Solve Your Child's Sleep Problems.* New York: Simon and Schuster.

Gandour, M. J. 1989. "Activity Level as a Dimension of Temperament in Toddlers: Its Relevance for the Organismic Specificity Hypothesis." *Child Development* 60: 1092–98.

Gaser, C., and G. Schlaug. 2003. "Brain Structures Differ between Musicians and Non-musicians." *Journal of Neuroscience* 23: 9240–45.

Gollwitzer, P. 1999. "Implementation Intentions: Strong Effects of Simple Plans." *American Psychologist* 57: 504–15.

Higgins, E. S. 2009. "Do ADHD Drugs Take a Toll on the Brain?" *Scientific American Mind*, July/August: 38–43.

Kern, L., G. J. DuPaul, R. J. Volpe, N. G. Sokol, J. G. Lutz, L. A. Arbolino, M. Pipan, and J. D. VanBrakle. 2007. "Multisetting Assessment–Based Intervention for Young Children at Risk for Attention Deficit Hyperactivity Disorder: Initial Effects on Academic and Behavioral Functioning." *School Psychology Review* 36: 237–55.

Kvols, K. J. 1998. *Redirecting Children's Behavior.* Seattle: Parenting Press.

Lecendreux, M., E. Konofal, M. Bouvard, B. Falissard, and M. C. Mouren-Simeoni. 2000. "Sleep and Alertness in Children with ADHD." *Association for Child Psychology and Psychiatry* 41: 803–12.

Lepper, M. R., D. Greene, and R. E. Nisbett. 1973. "Undermining Children's Intrinsic Interest with Extrinsic Rewards: A Test of the Over-Justification Hypothesis." *Journal of Personality and Social Psychology* 28: 139–87.

Martin, D. J., J. P. Garske, and M. K. Davis. 2000. "Relation of the Therapeutic Alliance with Outcome and Other Variables." *Journal of Consulting and Clinical Psychology* 68: 438–50.

Moffitt, T. E., L. Arseneault, D. Belsky, N. Dickson, R. J. Hancox, H. Harrington, et al. 2011. "A Gradient of Childhood Self-Control Predicts Health, Wealth, and Public Safety." *Proceedings of the National Academy of Sciences of the United States of America* 108: 2693–98.

Monastra, V. 2005. *Parenting Children with ADHD: 10 Lessons That Medicine Cannot Teach*. Washington, DC: American Psychological Association.

MTA Cooperative Group. 1999. "Moderators and Mediators of Treatment Response for Children with Attention-Deficit/Hyperactivity Disorder: The Multimodal Treatment Study of Children with Attention-Deficit/Hyperactivity Disorder." *Archives of General Psychiatry* 56: 1088–96.

———. 2004. "National Institute of Mental Health Multimodal Treatment Study of ADHD Follow-Up: Changes in Effectiveness and Growth after the End of Treatment." *Pediatrics* 113: 762–69.

Munsey, C. 2008. "New Insights on ADHD Treatment." *Monitor on Psychology* 39: 11.

Murphy, K. R., and M. Gordon. 1998. "Assessment of Adults with ADHD." In *Attention Deficit Hyperactivity Disorder: A Handbook for Diagnosis and Treatment*, 2nd ed., edited by R. A. Barkley. New York: Guilford Press.

Nelsen, J. 1987. *Positive Discipline*. New York: Ballantine.

Newcomer, L. L., and T. J. Lewis. 2004. "Functional Behavioral Assessment: An Investigation of Assessment Reliability and Effectiveness of Function-Based Interventions." *Journal of Emotional and Behavioral Disorders* 12: 168–81.

Nigg, J. T., H. H. Goldsmith, and J. Sacheck. 2004. "Temperament and Attention Deficit Hyperactivity Disorder: The Development of a

Multiple Pathway Model." *Journal of Clinical Child and Adolescent Psychology* 33: 42–53.

Pelham, W. 2007. "ADHD Drugs Not the Answer." *BBC News*, Nov. 12.

Pfiffner, L. J., and R. A. Barkley. 1998. "Treatment of ADHD in School Settings." In *Attention Deficit Hyperactivity Disorder: A Handbook for Diagnosis and Treatment*, 2nd ed., edited by R. A. Barkley. New York: Guilford Press.

Rappley, M. D. 2006. "Actual Psychotropic Medication Use in Preschool Children." *Infants and Young Children* 19: 154–63.

Robin, A. L. 2006. "Training Families with Adolescents with ADHD." In *Attention Deficit Hyperactivity Disorder: A Handbook for Diagnosis and Treatment*, 3rd ed., edited by R. A. Barkley. New York: Guilford Press.

Roizen, N. J., T. A. Blondis, M. Irwin, and M. Stein. 1994. "Adaptive Functioning in Children with Attention Deficit Hyperactivity Disorder." *Archives of Pediatric and Adolescent Medicine* 148: 1137–42.

Rosenthal, R. 1987. "Pygmalion Effects: Existence, Magnitude, and Social Importance." *Educational Researcher* 16: 37–41.

Spencer, T. J., J. Biederman, and T. Wilens. 1998. "Pharmacotherapy of ADHD with Antidepressants." In *Attention Deficit Hyperactivity Disorder: A Handbook for Diagnosis and Treatment*, 2nd ed., edited by R. A. Barkley. New York: Guilford Press.

Sroufe, L. A. 2005. Attachment and Development: A Prospective, Longitudinal Study from Birth to Adulthood. *Attachment and Human Development* 7: 349–367.

Twain, M. 1897. *Following the Equator: A Journey around the World*. Hartford, CT: American Publishing.

Wright, K. 2001. "Can Custom-Made Video Games Help Kids with Attention Deficit Disorder?" *Discover*, March. http://discover magazine.com/2001/mar/featworks/March 1, 2011.

Craig B. Wiener, EdD, has worked for over thirty years to help individuals diagnosed with attention deficit/hyperactivity disorder. He is a licensed psychologist and faculty member in the Department of Family Medicine and Community Health at the University of Massachusetts Medical School. His years as clinical director of outpatient mental health at the Family Health Center of Worcester and clinical experience in private practice led him to create a unique approach that identifies the factors that contribute to the reinforcement of ADHD behaviors. He lives in Worcester, MA.

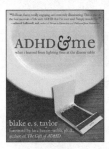

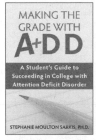